Retrospective Series on Critical Issues in Emotional/Behavioral Disorders

Improving the Social Skills of Children and Youth With Emotional/Behavioral Disorders

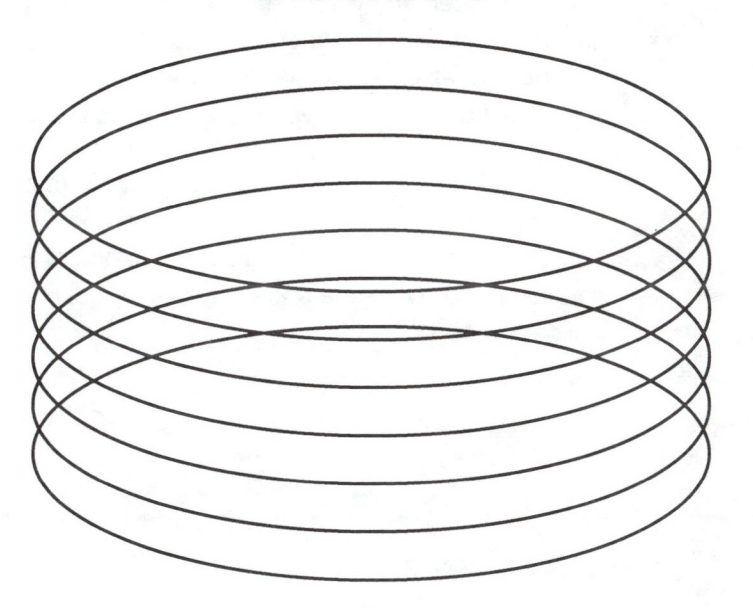

Lyndal M. Bullock, Robert A. Gable, Robert B. Rutherford, Jr.
Series Editors

The Council for Children with Behavioral Disorders

1996

Council for
Children with
Behavioral
Disorders

About the Council for Children with Behavioral Disorders (CCBD)

CCBD is an international professional organization committed to promoting and facilitating the education and general welfare of children/youth with behavioral and emotional disorders. CCBD, whose members include educators, parents, mental health personnel, and a variety of other professionals, actively pursues quality educational services and program alternatives for persons with behavioral disorders, advocates for the needs of such children and youth, emphasizes research and professional growth as vehicles for better understanding behavioral disorders, and provides professional support for persons who are involved with and serve children and youth with behavioral disorders.

In advocating for the professionals in the field of behavioral disorders, CCBD (a division of The Council for Exceptional Children) endorses the Standards for Professional Practice and Code of Ethics which was adopted by the Delegate Assembly of The Council for Exceptional Children in 1983.

ISBN 0-86586-283-4

CEC Stock No. D5158

Copyright © 1996 by the Council for Children with Behavioral Disorders, a Division of The Council for Exceptional Children, 1920 Association Drive, Reston, VA 22091.

Printed in the United States of America

Contents

Foreword v

Analysis of Literature on Social Competence
of Behaviorally Disordered Children and Youth 1
    Sarup R. Mathur and Robert B. Rutherford, Jr.

A Validation of Social Skills for Students with
Behavioral Disorders 13
    Nancy Meadows, Richard S. Neel, Gerilyn Parker
    and Kimberly Timo

Social Interaction Research and Families
of Behaviorally Disordered Children:
A Critical Review and Forward Look 27
    James Fox and Sarah Savelle

Structured Learning: A Psychoeducational Approach for
Teaching Social Competencies 47
    Arnold P. Goldstein, Robert P. Sprafkin, Jane Gershaw
    and Paul Klein

Use of Cognitive Mediation Strategies for Social Skills
Training: Theoretical and Conceptual Issues 59
    John W. Maag

Using a Peer Confrontation System
in a Group Setting 73
    Spencer J. Salend, Nancy Reid Jantzen, and Karen Giek

Social Interaction Training for Preschool Children
with Behavioral Disorders 83
    Mary A. McEvoy and Samuel L. Odom

Entrapment Effects and the Generalization and Maintenance
of Social Skills Training for Elementary School Students with
Behavioral Disorders 95
    Scott R. McConnell

Structured Learning Using Self-Monitoring to Promote
Maintenance and Generalization of Social Skills Across
Settings for a Behaviorally Disordered Adolescent 111
    Cheryl Strobel Kiburz, Sidney R. Miller, and Lonny W. Morrow

Foreword

This is the first in a series of monographs containing articles previously published by the Council for Children with Behavioral Disorders (CCBD). The topics that together comprise the series have been identified by CCBD members as among the most critical in dealing with children and youth with emotional/behavioral disorders. This volume is devoted to the issue of social skills.

Retrospective Series on Critical Issues in Emotional/Behavioral Disorders

There is little doubt that an intact repertoire of prosocial skills is indispensable to normal growth and development. In contrast, a diminished capacity to initiate and sustain positive social interactions can have ruinous effects on life span adjustment. Unfortunately, both accumulated research and classroom experience substantiate that many students categorized as seriously emotionally disturbed, emotionally handicapped, or behaviorally disordered are deficient in the critical area of social skills.

In this volume, we have attempted to provide a selection of readings that not only stand alone on merit but also share a common purpose—to furnish practitioners with the tools to improve the social skills of students with emotional/behavioral disorders.

Lyndal M. Bullock
Robert A. Gable
Robert B. Rutherford, Jr.
Series Editors

Analysis of Literature on Social Competence of Behaviorally Disordered Children and Youth

Sarup R. Mathur
Robert B. Rutherford, Jr.

ABSTRACT: The present review has been conducted to critically evaluate recent intervention research on the social competence of behaviorally disordered children and adolescents. The purpose of this review was to analyze the concept of social competence and to evaluate the efficacy of intervention procedures used in the literature. The results of the review indicate that (a) research has failed to build a comprehensive conceptual base for social competence, (b) interventions have resulted in positive behavioral change, and (c) generalization of behavior across time, stimuli, and responses needs to be improved.

Social competence can be defined as having the social skills necessary to interact in socially acceptable ways. Behaviorally disordered children often demonstrate lack of appropriate social behaviors. Frequently, this results in social rejection by peers which further hampers the success of mainstreaming (Gresham, 1982). Rejected children report feelings of extreme loneliness (Asher & Wheeler, 1985) and they often are at-risk for delinquency and psychosocial adjustment problems (Cowen, Pederson, Babigian, Izzo, & Trost, 1973; Roff, Sells, & Golden, 1972).

To improve the social acceptance of behaviorally disordered children in mainstream settings, social skills instruction is essential. Preparation for social integration should be a necessary part of their educational program (Hollinger, 1987). If these students had acquired functional social competence, they probably would not have been classified as behaviorally disordered. Regular classroom placement of a behaviorally disordered student without providing training to enhance social competence is asking for failure. Available literature suggests that social skills training is a viable intervention to increase the successful mainstreaming of behaviorally disordered children (LaNunziata, Hill, & Krause, 1981).

The purpose of this article is to (a) analyze the conceptual framework of social competence, (b) analyze different approaches proposed for social skills training that enhance social competence of behaviorally disordered children, and (c) critically evaluate the success of these interventions in terms of promoting generalization.

> There is a great variability in how social competence and social skills are defined; social competence and social skills do not imply the same concept.

The present review focuses on the past 5 years of social competence research with behaviorally disordered children and youth. It builds on an earlier review conducted by Schloss, Schloss, Wood, and Kiehl (1986) which analyzed 25 social skills studies with behaviorally disordered students. The present review analyzed 17 additional published articles on social competence/social skills interventions.

CONCEPTUAL FRAMEWORK

Much attention has been given recently to training behaviorally disordered children and youth in social skills, but not to developing a sound conceptual base of what constitutes social competence (Gresham, 1986; Gresham & Elliott, 1987; Hollinger, 1987). Indeed, there is a great variability in how social competence and social skills are defined; social competence and social skills do not imply the same concept. Social skills are specific behaviors necessary for an individual to perform a task competently. In contrast, social competence represents an evaluative term based upon judgments—given certain criteria that a person has adequately performed a task (Gresham, 1986; McFall, 1982).

Social Competence

Although social competence encompasses a wide area of cognitive and behavioral skills, generally the term refers to a person's effective participation in a social setting. The term social competence has been defined in many ways that reflect the varying perspectives of social theorists. Some theorists have defined it as a combination of adaptive behavior and social skills (Gresham & Elliott, 1987; Leland, 1978), while others have viewed it in terms of social interaction and social reciprocity (Gaylord-Ross & Haring, 1987; Hollinger, 1987). Meichenbaum, Butler, and Gruson (1981) presented a theoretical model of social competence based on a cognitive behavior modification paradigm that contends a focus on overt behaviors is necessary but not sufficient in studying social competence. Meichenbaum and his colleagues assert that the role of cognitive process also must be taken into account in viewing social competence as a construct. From this perspective, the acquisition of social competence depends upon an individual's cognitive awareness of his or her social situation.

These definitions reveal differences in their relative emphasis. These differences may be best considered as semantic disagreements, because each of these definitions refers to separate constructs that may or may not empirically relate to each other.

Social Skills

Social skills are viewed as part of the global construct known as social competence. Gresham (1986) has described three types of social skills comprising social competence which include (a) peer acceptance, (b) behavioral skills, and (c) social validity. Peer acceptance involves measuring peer acceptability or popularity to define children as socially skilled. Few of the studies reviewed focused upon the peer acceptance definition or used sociometric assessment to evaluate the effectiveness of interventions (Bierman, 1986; Sainato, Maheady, & Shook, 1986; Tiffen & Spence, 1986).

When social skills are defined as situationally specific observable behaviors, the antecedents and consequences of the particular social behaviors are identified, specified, and operationalized for the purpose of assessment and intervention. Many researchers have addressed social skills in behavioral terms. The behavioral definitions of social skills include: increasing rate of social initiation (Fox, Shores, Lindeman, & Strain, 1986), communicative interaction (Bierman, 1986; Goldstein & Wickstrom, 1986), sharing, play organization (Odom & Strain, 1986), eye contact, facial expression, body posture, voice tone, and giving and following instructions (Serna, Schumaker, Hazel, & Sheldon, 1986). Although behavioral definitions identify the particular social behaviors, the social validity of these behaviors has not been ascertained.

The social validity definition not only specifies behaviors in which the child is deficient but also defines these behaviors as socially skilled, based upon their relationship to socially important outcomes. Two studies in the present review mentioned employing social validation measures to demonstrate the effectiveness of intervention (Christoff et al., 1985; Serna et al., 1986).

Definitions which are premised on the global aspects of maladaptive behavior in terms of social skills deficits are of limited usefulness because of their lack of specificity. Rather, they become ambiguous and complex. The field needs a definition that incorporates a balance between being too global or too molecular.

Theoretical Basis

There are two main reasons for the lack of a sound conceptual base of social competence: a lack of appropriate definition, and a unified theory of social competence that is both practical and coherent. A theoretical conceptualization of social competence emphasizing adaptive behavior was developed by Leland (1978). Adaptive behavior is comprised of three components: (a) independent functioning, (b) personal responsibility, and (c) social responsibility. A socially responsible and socially skilled individual performs appropriate behavior in terms of societal expectations. Due to the lack of empirical data support, the validity of Leland's (1978) conceptualization is still in question.

In contrast to Leland's perspective, Hollinger (1987) proposed a more balanced concept which incorporates both molar and molecular levels of analysis of social competence. From the molecular perspective, the analysis focuses on observable behaviors, which entails an understanding of the specific behaviors or social skills comprising social competence. In contrast, the molar perspective focuses on broad dimensional analysis of social competence.

More recently, Gresham and Elliott (1987) conceptualized social competence as being comprised of two interrelated components: adaptive behavior and social skills. The effectiveness and degree to which an individual meets social/cultural standards of personal independence and social responsibility is reflective of the adaptive behavior. According to Gresham and Elliott, an adaptive behavior includes independent functioning skills, physical development, language development, and academic competencies. Social skills represent behaviors which in specific situations predict important social outcomes. Due to a failure to provide clear distinctions between adaptive behavior and social skill, the explicitness of this conceptualization is limited.

A recent concept in the field of social competence is entrapment of behavior (McConnell, 1987). Entrapment is described as a process through which the social behavior of a child comes under the control of naturally occurring reinforcers. This can occur when changes in the social behavior

> There are two main reasons for the lack of a sound conceptual base of social competence: a lack of appropriate definition, and a unified theory of social competence that is both practical and coherent.

> Contemporary research on intervention procedures reveals two main approaches of developing social competence: social skills training and social problem solving.

of the child are reinforced by the social behavior of others during interactions in naturalistic settings. As a result, social skills develop through an elaboration of these behaviors. However, to facilitate the entrapment of social interaction, attention is required to the selection of target behavior and the use of intervention procedures.

Viewed together, these aforementioned conceptualizations represent diverse views of the construct of social competence. However, a cohesiveness noted within the diversity of views is the perception of social competence as a global judgment of a person's adequate social functioning. Along with developing a conceptual framework for social competence, it is important to consider how social skills that constitute social competence are taught to behaviorally disordered children.

INTERVENTION RESEARCH

To examine the effectiveness of intervention procedures in promoting the social competence of behaviorally disordered children and youth, 17 articles relating to intervention research were reviewed. Each of these studies was analyzed according to the components developed by Schloss et al. (1986) which include subjects, target behavior, and procedures employed. In addition, setting, experimental design, and results were included in the present analysis (see Table 1).

Major Intervention Approaches

Contemporary research on intervention procedures revealed two main approaches of developing social competence. One approach focuses on systematic teaching of specific prosocial behaviors to behaviorally disordered children, and is referred to as social skills training. This approach employs direct instruction, modeling, prompting, rehearsal of specific social skills, and positive reinforcement.

A study conducted by Bierman (1986) illustrates this approach. Participating in the study were 27 preadolescents who were perceived as unpopular and lacking conversational skills. Each of these subjects engaged in cooperative activities with two socially accepted classmates. Half of these triads received coaching in social conversation skills, while the others received nonspecific adult support. Children who received social skills training displayed more conversational skills and received more peer support. Similar improvement in target behaviors of behaviorally disordered children as a result of social skills training has been documented in several other studies (Goldstein & Wickstrom, 1986; Kohler & Fowler, 1985; Tiffen & Spence, 1986).

A second approach to developing social competence identified in the present review focuses on social cognitive processes and is referred to as social problem-solving. For example, Spivack and his colleagues (Spivack, Platt, & Shure, 1976; Spivack & Shure, 1974) initiated the use of this approach in their studies. These studies reported that children who received training in interpersonal cognitive problem-solving increased their abilities to generate alternative solutions and anticipate consequences.

In the past, social problem-solving was considered to be a promising technique for normal samples (without handicaps) as a preventive means of fostering social competence. However, a recent trend in the application of problem-solving interventions has occurred with clinical populations. A tentative evidence exists for its effect on acquisition of social skills with shy (Christoff et. al., 1985) and aggressive (Dubow, Huesmann, & Eron, 1987; Vaughn, Ridley, & Bullock, 1984) children. Success of this approach has also been demonstrated with severely emotionally disturbed children (Amis, Gesten, Smith, Clark, & Stark, 1988; Yu, Harris, Solovitz, & Franklin, 1986).

Yu et al. (1986) employed a social problem-solving (SPS) procedure with 7- to 12-year-old boys who were child psychiatric outpatients demonstrating behavioral problems. The results demonstrated that SPS trained youngsters generated more problem solutions and showed greater reductions in acting out behaviors relative to those under traditional psychotherapy treatment. Similar findings were obtained by Vaughn et al. (1984) using a social problem-solving intervention with aggressive children.

Of the 17 studies reviewed, 12 employed social skills training while 5 studies used a problem-solving training procedure, either by itself or along with other procedures. Dubow et al. (1987) compared the effectiveness of cognitive training, behavioral training, cognitive-behavioral training, and play training. The results indicated that the children receiving cognitive-behavioral and play interventions significantly decreased aggressive behavior and increased prosocial behaviors than did those exposed to either cognitive or behavioral training alone.

In general, the studies reviewed that employed a social problem-solving or social skills training approach produced positive results. However, some of the authors indicated limited success because intervention did not result in positive behavior change in all the subjects or in all the target behaviors (Amish et al., 1988; Sasso, Mitchell, & Struthers, 1986; Serna et al., 1986; Tiffen & Spence, 1985; Yu et al., 1986).

Peer-Mediated Interventions

Recently, researchers have begun to investigate the use of peer-mediated approaches to increasing social competence (Brady et al., 1984; Brady, Shores, McEvoy, Ellis, & Fox, 1987; Goldstein & Wickstrom, 1986; Gunter, Fox, Brady, Shores, & Cavanaugh, 1988; Kohler & Fowler, 1985, Odom & Strain, 1986; Sasso et al., 1986).

Odom and Strain (1986), for example, compared the relative effectiveness of peer-initiated and teacher-antecedent interventions with autistic children. In the peer-initiation condition, confederates were taught to initiate interaction with the autistic children, whereas in the teacher-antecedent condition teachers prompted the autistic children to initiate with confederates who had been taught to reciprocate. During the teacher-antecedent condition, children's social initiations and responses increased, and longer chains of social interactions were noticed. The peer-initiation procedure also reliably increased the social responses of autistic children.

Goldstein and Wickstrom (1986) demonstrated success with three behaviorally disordered preschool children using peer-mediated intervention. The intervention resulted in higher rates of interaction that stayed above baseline levels during the maintenance condition for each of the children.

Peer-mediated interventions are based on the assumption that children develop social skills through their interactions with peers (Hollinger, 1987; Kohler & Fowler, 1985). Learning a particular prosocial behavior in the presence of peers provides a natural environment which may facilitate maintenance and

> Peer-mediated interventions are based on the assumption that children develop social skills through their interactions with peers.

Table 1

Qualitative Aspects of Intervention Research Focusing on

Citations	Subjects	Setting	Target Behaviors
Amish, Gesten, Smith, Clark, & Stark (1988)	25 severely emotionally disturbed children	School	Problem-solving skills, social adjustment
Bierman (1986)	27 unpopular children with conversational problems	School	Conversational skills, positive peer responses
Brady, Shores, Gunter, McEvoy, Fox, & White (1984)	1 autistic adolescent boy	School	Social interaction
Brady, Shores, McEvoy, Ellis, & Fox (1987)	2 autistic children	School	Social interaction
Christoff, Scott, Kelly, Schlundt, Baer, & Kelly (1985)	6 shy preadolescents	School	Problem-solving skills, conversational skills
Dubow, Huesmann, & Eron (1987)	104 aggressive boys	School	Promote prosocial behavior, decrease aggression
Fox, Shores, Lindeman, & Strain (1986)	3 withdrawn preschool children	School	Social initiations, peer responses
Goldstein & Wickstrom (1986)	3 behaviorally disordered, language-delayed preschool children	School	Communicative interaction
Gunter, Fox, Brady, Shores, & Cavanaugh (1988)	2 socially withdrawn autistic boys	School	Social interaction initiation, soliciting response
Kohler & Fowler (1985)	3 young girls with behavior problems	School	Prosocial responses
Odom & Strain (1986)	3 preschool autistic boys	School	Social initiation, responses
Sainato, Maheady, & Shook (1986)	3 socially withdrawn kindergarten children	School	Social interaction, sociometric standing
Sasso, Mitchell, & Struthers (1986)	4 autistic, 4 nonhandicapped children	School	Cooperative interaction, instructional interaction
Serna, Schumaker, Hazel, & Sheldon (1986)	12 behavior-problem adolescents and 6 parents	County juvenile court office	Youth skills, parent skills, youth parent interaction skills
Tiffen & Spence (1986)	25 isolated and 25 rejected children	School	Social competence
Vaughn, Ridley, & Bullock (1984)	24 aggressive children	School	Problem-solving behavior
Yu, Harris, Solovitz, & Franklin (1986)	35 behaviorally disordered boys	Clinic	Social cognitive skills, behavioral adjustment

Behaviorally Disordered Children and Youth from 1984 to 1988

Procedures	Experimental Design	Result
Instruction, discussion, modeling, role-play, feedback	Group study	SPS trained subjects generated more solutions
Social skill training, peer experience	Group study	Increase in social skill performance
Instructions, modeling, physical guidance, prompting	Multiple baseline across peers	Increase in social interaction
Multiple peer exemplar training	Multiple baseline across peers	Generalized behavior change in one subject
Problem-solving, conversation training, group training	Multiple baseline across skills	Improvement in target skills
Cognitive training, behavioral training, combined training, attention/play training	Group study	Positive results in combined and attention/play training
Prompting, praising, fading	Withdrawal, multiple baseline across subjects	Increase in social interaction of 2 children
Direct instruction, peer training, teacher prompting	Multiple baseline across subjects	Increase in target behavior
Prompt, praise	Multiple baseline across peers	Increase in target behavior in one subject
Peer training, group contingency, modeling, rehearsal, feedback	Multiple baseline across behavior and reversal	Positive effects on interaction
Peer-initiated intervention, teacher-antecedent intervention	Alternating treatment design	Differential effects of interventions
Role-play, environmental manipulation	Multiple baseline across subjects	Positive results in both target behaviors
Peer-tutoring, structured interaction activities	Inverted design	Structured interaction more effective than tutoring
Reciprocal social skill training	Multiple baseline across skills, control group design	Overall improvements in each of the trained skills areas
Instruction, discussion, modeling, role-play, feedback, social reinforcement	Group study	Failed to produce the effectiveness of SST
Role-play, practice, teaching language concepts, cue sensitivity, goal identification	Group study	Increase in target behavior
Social problem-solving, role-play group discussions, drawing projects, parental involvement	Group study	Increase in social cognitive skills

> An important consideration in judging the success of an intervention relates to the extent of behavioral generalization.

generalization of the newly learned behavior. Conducting social skills training in the peer group may be an effective way of addressing the social adjustment problems faced by mainstreamed behaviorally disordered children. Although there is evidence that various groups of behaviorally disordered children benefit from these interventions, it appears that particularly withdrawn and autistic children, because of their often limited language skills, would benefit most from peer-mediated interventions (Brady et al., 1984; Brady et al., 1987; Goldstein & Wickstrom, 1986; Gunter et al., 1988).

GENERALIZATION

An important consideration in judging the success of an intervention relates to the extent of behavioral generalization (e.g., Baer, Wolf, & Risley, 1968). Behavioral researchers have addressed the difficulties in achieving durable behavior change (Keeley, Shemberg, & Carbonell, 1976; Stokes & Baer, 1977). More recently, Rutherford and Nelson (1988) found in their review of literature that less than 2% of the approximately 5,300 articles published in the journals from 1977 to 1988 contained studies that addressed maintenance and generalization of educational treatment effects, and less than 1% contained studies that systematically programmed for maintenance and generalization of these effects across settings, responses, trainers, or time.

Following the format developed by Schloss et al. (1986), the 17 articles reviewed in the present study were analyzed with regard to the extent that stimulus generalization, response generalization, and generalization over time were tested or programmed and whether these forms of generalization were found (Table 2).

The findings of the present review that relate to generalization effects indicate that improvement is needed in achieving generalization of socially competent behavior across time, stimuli, and responses. Of the 17 intervention research studies reported in Table 2, only 10 included evidence of programming for stimulus generalization, with only 9 showing positive results. Response generalization was reported to be measured in 8 studies, of which 7 showed favorable results. And 12 studies included follow-up data to indicate maintenance of results over time.

Generalization strategies included the use of nontraining settings to transfer and maintain performance (Gunter et al., 1988); nonintrusive use of prompting to promote target behaviors (Goldstein & Wickstrom, 1986); response-dependent fading of stimuli (Fox et al., 1986); group-oriented contingencies (Kohler & Fowler, 1985); peer reciprocity and peer entrapment (Kohler & Fowler, 1985); overlearning of material (Amish et al., 1988); developing problem-solving skills (Yu et al., 1986); and systematic inclusion of parental involvement (Serna et al., 1986). Multiple peer exemplar training also appeared to be a viable component of generalization programming (Brady et al., 1987; Gunter et al., 1988).

Despite the small number of studies that indicated generality and maintenance of effects, the literature reveals an overall development of generalization technology (Rutherford & Nelson, 1988).

CONCLUSION

There is strong evidence suggesting the effectiveness of social skills interventions with behaviorally disordered children and youth. However, there are several critical limitations apparent in the literature including a lack of comprehensive

Table 2
Generalization and Maintenance Results

Citations	Stimulus Generalization Programmed	Stimulus Generalization Found	Response Generalization Programmed	Response Generalization Found	Generalization Over Time Programmed	Generalization Over Time Found
Amish, Gesten, Smith, Clark, & Stark (1988)	No	No	Yes	No	No	No
Bierman (1986)	Yes	Yes	No	No	6 weeks	Yes
Brady, Shores, Gunter, McEvoy, Fox, & White (1984)	Yes	Yes	Yes	Yes	37-46 days	Some
Brady, Shores, McEvoy, Ellis, & Fox (1987)	Yes	Yes with one subject	Yes	Yes with one subject	44-56 days	Yes with one subject
Christoff, Scott, Kelly, Schlundt, Baer, & Kelly (1985)	Yes	No	Yes	Yes	5 months	Yes
Dubow, Huesmann, & Eron (1987)	No	No	No	No	6 months	Some
Fox, Shores, Lindeman, & Strain (1986)	Yes	Yes	Yes	Yes	2½ months for 2 subjects	Yes
Goldstein & Wickstrom (1986)	Yes	Yes	No	No	5-8 weeks	Yes
Gunter, Fox, Brady, Shores, & Cavanaugh (1988)	Yes	Yes for one subject	Yes	Yes	No	No
Kohler & Fowler (1985)	Yes	Yes	No	No	4 weeks for one subject	Some
Odom & Strain (1986)	No	No	No	No	No	No
Sainato, Maheady, & Shook (1986)	No	No	Yes	Yes	4 weeks	Some
Sasso, Mitchell, & Struthers (1986)	Yes	Yes	No	No	No	No
Serna, Schumaker, Hazel, & Sheldon (1986)	No	No	No	No	10 months	Yes
Tiffen & Spence (1986)	No	No	No	No	3 months	Yes
Vaughn, Ridley, & Bullock (1984)	No	No	No	No	3 months	Yes
Yu, Harris, Solovitz, & Franklin (1986)	Yes	Yes	Yes	Yes	No	No

> Most of the research in the area of social skills has focused upon changes in specific behaviors without considering their social utility in context.

conceptual framework of social competence, a lack of social validation of interventions, and insufficient generalization.

The results of the review by Schloss et al. (1986) indicate several limitations existing in the literature to include: (a) a lack of comprehensive conceptualization, (b) a lack of social importance of training effects, (c) poorly defined and inconsistently applied training tactics which decreases the likelihood of replication of research, and (d) failure to demonstrate generalization across settings, responses, and time. The results of the present review are in agreement with the aforementioned findings of Schloss et al. (1986).

The field remains limited in terms of a general conceptual framework of social competence. Researchers are using their own idiosyncratic definitions to define almost any behavior as a social skill (Gresham, 1986). In the studies reviewed, target behaviors included eye contact, loudness of speech, giving and receiving compliments, social initiation, conversational skills, social adjustment, listening to instructions, and so forth. The purpose of response discrete definition is to operationalize the behavior which further enhances the possibility of the replication of the study. However, the disadvantages of focusing on discrete response definitions include: (a) an emphasis on isolated responses in which global conceptual systems are disregarded (Schloss et al., 1986), (b) limited social validity of behavior, and (c) limited generalization of behavior. We need a conceptual system which is broad enough to incorporate both precision in evaluation and wide range of behavior.

With some notable exceptions, most of the research in the area of social skills has focused upon changes in specific behaviors without considering their social utility in context. Future research should be directed at assessing those specific behaviors that are best predictors of an individual's standing on important social outcomes (Gresham, 1986).

Simply teaching a specific prosocial behavior or strategy of social behavior to increase the quantity of behavior is generally not the goal of social competence training. The goal is to demonstrate the long-term maintenance and generalization of the desired social behavioral changes of behaviorally disordered children (Stokes & Baer, 1977).

Appropriate social behaviors must continue after intervention ceases and behavior must occur outside the training settings. Although much success has been noted with developing social competence of behaviorally disordered children, the limited ability of social skills training to produce generalizable changes in behavior raises the question of how training procedures can be improved.

REFERENCES

Amish, P. L., Gesten, E. L., Smith, H. B., Clark, H. B., & Stark, C. (1988). Social problem-solving training for severely emotionally and behaviorally disturbed children. *Behavioral Disorders, 13,* 175-186.

Asher, S. R., & Wheeler, V. A. (1985). Children's loneliness: A comparison of rejected and neglected peer status. *Journal of Consulting and Clinical Psychology, 53,* 500-505.

Baer, D. M., Wolf, M. M., & Risley, T. R. (1968). Some current dimensions of applied behavior analysis. *Journal of Applied Behavior Analysis, 1,* 91-97.

Bierman, K. L. (1986). Process of change during social skills training with preadolescents and its relation to treatment outcome. *Child Development, 57,* 230-240.

Brady, M. P., Shores, R. E., Gunter, R., McEvoy, M. A., Fox, J. J., & White, C. (1984). Generalization of an adolescent's social interaction behavior via multiple peers in a classroom. *Journal of the Association for Persons with Severe Handicaps, 9,* 278-286.

Brady, M. P., Shores, R. E., McEvoy, M. A., Ellis, D., & Fox, J. J. (1987). Increasing social interaction of severely handicapped autistic children. *Journal of Autism and Developmental Disorders, 17,* 375-390.

Christoff, K. A., Scott, W. N., Kelly, M. L., Schlundt, D., Baer, G., & Kelly, J. A. (1985). Social skills and social problem-solving training for shy young adolescents. *Behavior Therapy, 16,* 468-477.

Cowen, E. L., Pederson, A., Babigian, H., Izzo, L. D., & Trost, M. A. (1973). Long-term follow-up of early detected vulnerable children. *Journal of Consulting and Clinical Psychology, 41,* 438-446.

Dubow, E. F., Huesmann, R., & Eron, L. D. (1987). Mitigating aggression and promoting prosocial behavior in aggressive elementary schoolboys. *Behavior Research Therapy, 25,* 527-531.

Fox, J. J., Shores, R. E., Lindeman, D., & Strain, P. S. (1986). Maintaining social initiations of withdrawn handicapped and nonhandicapped preschoolers through a response dependent fading tactic. *Journal of Abnormal Child Psychology, 14,* 387-396.

Gaylord-Ross, R., & Haring, T. (1987). Social interaction research for adolescents with severe handicaps. *Behavioral Disorders, 12,* 264-275.

Goldstein, H., & Wickstrom, S. (1986). Peer intervention effects on communicative interaction among handicapped and nonhandicapped preschoolers. *Journal of Applied Behavior Analysis, 19,* 209-214.

Gresham, F. M. (1982). Misguided mainstreaming: The case for social skills training with handicapped children. *Exceptional Children, 48,* 422-433.

Gresham, F. M. (1986). Conceptual and definitional issues in the assessment of children's social skills: Implications for classification and training. *Journal of Clinical Child Psychology, 15,* 3-15.

Gresham, F. M., & Elliott, S. N. (1987). The relationship between adaptive behavior and social skills: Issues in definition and assessment. *Journal of Special Education, 21,* 167-181.

Gunter, P., Fox, J. J., Brady, M. P., Shores, R. E., & Cavanaugh, K. (1988). Nonhandicapped peers as multiple exemplars: A generalization tactic for promoting autistic students' social skills. *Behavioral Disorders, 13,* 116-126.

Hollinger, J. D. (1987). Social skills for behaviorally disordered children as preparation for mainstreaming: Theory, practice, and new directions. *Remedial and Special Education, 8,* 17-27.

Keeley, S. M., Shemberg, K. M., & Carbonell, J. (1976). Operant clinical intervention: Behavior management or beyond? Where are the data? *Behavior Therapy, 7,* 292-305.

Kohler, F., & Fowler, S. A. (1985). Training prosocial behaviors to young children: An analysis of reciprocity with untrained peers. *Journal of Applied Behavior Analysis, 18,* 187-200.

LaNunziata, L. J., Hill, D. S., & Krause, L. A. (1981). Teaching social skills in classrooms for behaviorally disordered students. *Behavioral Disorders, 6,* 238-246.

LeLand, H. (1978). Theoretical considerations of adaptive behavior. In A. Coulter & H. Morrow (Eds.), *Adaptive behavior: Concepts and measurements* (pp. 21-44). New York: Grune & Stratton.

McConnell, S. R. (1987). Entrapment effects and the generalization and maintenance of social skills training for elementary school students with behavioral disorders. *Behavioral Disorders, 12,* 252-263.

McFall, R. M. (1982). A review and reformulation of the concept of social skills. *Behavioral Assessment, 4,* 1-33.

Meichenbaum, D., Butler, L., & Gruson, L. (1981). Toward a conceptual model of social competence. In J. D. Wine & M. D. Smye (Eds.), *Social competence.* New York: Guilford.

Odom, S. L., & Strain, P. S. (1986). A comparison of peer-initiation and teacher antecedent interventions for promoting reciprocal social interaction of autistic preschoolers. *Journal of Applied Behavior Analysis, 19,* 59-71.

Roff, M., Sells, B., & Golden, M. (1972). *Social adjustment and personality development in children.* Minneapolis: University of Minnesota Press.

Rutherford, R. B., Jr., & Nelson, C. M. (1988). Generalization and maintenance of treatment effects. In J. C. Witt, S. N. Elliott, & F. M. Gresham (Eds.), *Handbook of Behavior Therapy in Education.* New York: Plenum.

Sainato, D. M., Maheady, L., & Shook, G. L. (1986). The effects of a classroom manager role on the social interaction patterns and social status of withdrawn kindergarten students. *Journal of Applied Behavior Analysis, 19,* 187-195.

Sasso, G. M., Mitchell, V. M., & Struthers, E. M. (1986). Peer tutoring versus structured interaction activities: Effects on the frequency and topography of peer initiations. *Behavioral Disorders, 11,* 249-259.

Schloss, P. J., Schloss, C. N., Wood, C. E., & Kiehl, W. S. (1986). A critical review of social skills research with behaviorally disordered students. *Behavioral Disorders, 12,* 1-14.

Serna, L. A., Schumaker, J. B., Hazel, J. S., & Sheldon, J. B. (1986). Teaching reciprocal social skills to parents and their delinquent adolescents. *Journal of Clinical Child Psychology, 15,* 64-77.

A Validation of Social Skills for Students with Behavioral Disorders

Nancy Meadows
Richard S. Neel
Gerilyn Parker
Kimberly Timo

ABSTRACT: Secondary students with behavioral disorders, regular education secondary students, secondary teachers of students with behavioral disorders, regular education secondary teachers, and parents of both student populations from the states of Washington, Iowa, and Colorado were asked to complete the Adolescent Social Skills Survey (Walker, Todis, Holmes, & Horton, 1988). The survey consists of 48 items about how adolescents relate to themselves, to other adolescents, and to adults. Overall, all groups thought all items on the survey were important. As a group, students with serious behavioral disorders rated interpersonal skills higher than other skills on the survey. However, these same students consistently rated all items lower. These students also rated compliance and cooperation skills as less important than the two teacher groups. Discussion centers around the implications these results have on programming for seriously behaviorally disordered students, with future needs being directed toward developing a functionally valid list of critical social skills.

Since the enactment of Public Law 94-142 and its mandate of "least restrictive environment," exceptional students have been mainstreamed into regular classrooms in greater numbers than ever before. Unfortunately, the physical placement of mildly handicapped children in the presence of their nonhandicapped peers has not resulted in mutual social interaction and acceptance between the two groups (Gresham, 1982; Sabornie, 1985). Research has shown that all handicapped students do not have the appropriate social skills to succeed in mainstream situations nor do they acquire the necessary social skills by modeling their nonhandicapped peers (Asher & Hymel, 1981; Cartledge, Frew, & Zaharias, 1985; Gresham, 1981, 1982). Moreover, studies have demonstrated that there are typically low rates of social interaction between mainstreamed handicapped children and their classmates (Bruininks, 1978; Gresham, 1981; Morgan, 1977).

For students with serious behavioral disorders, social skill deficiencies may be the most critical deterrent to social acceptance (Schloss, Schloss, Wood, & Kiehl, 1986). By definition, these students are set apart by their lack of social competence. Numerous studies have indicated that (a)

Reprinted from *Behavioral Disorders*, Vol. 16, Number 3, May 1991, pp. 200-210

> Investigation of current instruction of social skills has provided mixed results, indicating that new social behaviors may be learned but they do not generalize across a variety of social situations and do not maintain after intervention is terminated.

students with behavioral disorders lack appropriate social skills (Gresham, 1982, 1986; Kauffman, 1989); (b) many students with behavior problems are poorly accepted by their peers (Asher & Hymel, 1981; Asher & Taylor, 1983; Gresham, 1986; Michelson & Wood, 1980; Sabornie, 1985); and (c) many students with behavioral disorders are rated by their teachers as having inadequate social skills (Gresham, 1982, 1986). These findings indicate that, prior to placing seriously behaviorally disordered students in mainstream classes, educators need to look more closely at students' specific social skills deficits and their levels of social competency.

It has been well documented in the literature that social skills have an important relationship to all aspects of students' lives: educational, social, and employment (Combs & Slaby, 1977; Gronlund & Anderson, 1962; Michelson & Wood, 1980; Roff, Sells, & Golden, 1972; Ullman, 1957). Furthermore, problems in these areas have long lasting effects. Adults who have documented social deficits as children are reported to have psychological problems (Gottman, Gonso, & Schuler, 1976; Sheperd, 1980), unsuccessful employment histories (Knold, 1985; Neel, Meadows, Levine, & Edgar, 1988), negative military service records (Roff, 1970), and increased incidences of suicide (Stengel, 1973). Psychologists, employers, and educators agree that early intervention should occur within the school setting in an attempt to counteract these problems (Gottman et al., 1976; Knold, 1985; Roff, 1970; Roff et al., 1972; Sheperd, 1980).

Investigation of current instruction of social skills has provided mixed results, indicating that new social behaviors may be learned but they do not generalize across a variety of social situations and do not maintain after intervention is terminated (Bellack, 1983; McConnell, 1987). Social skills training programs have not produced behavioral changes that make handicapped children more socially acceptable (Kauffman, 1989).

One of the reasons suggested for the lack of success of social skills programs is that the skills targeted for instruction may not be those which will lead to positive social exchanges. As Kauffman (1989) states, "The goal of intervention must be to help the socially isolated individual become enmeshed or entrapped in positive, reciprocal, self-perpetuating social exchanges, which can be done only by carefully choosing the target skills" (p. 336). Target skills must relate to peers or other important people in the environment (teacher, parents, other adults) where they will encounter naturally occurring prompts and reinforcers (McConnell, 1987). It is important to teach skills that are valued not only by the individual student but also by others in his or her environment.

The social skills currently targeted for instruction may not be those which are socially valid for students. Current social skills programs have focused on those skills which adults, not students themselves, have judged important (Kazdin & Matson, 1981; LeCroy, 1983). As a result, socially incompetent students may not increase their levels of social acceptance even if specific skills are mastered.

Kazdin and Matson (1981) have suggested subjective evaluation as one method for establishing the validity of training targets. This involves obtaining feedback from significant others to establish social significance of target behaviors. If the social skill acquired is not valued by others in the learner's environment, social competence in those settings will not be increased. The identification of functional social skills—skills which will increase a child's competence in the classroom, with peers, with teachers, and with other adults—is urgently needed.

The purpose of this study was to take a closer look at the social skills which have been targeted for intervention and to determine if the particular needs of seriously behaviorally disordered students have been addressed. Extending the work of Williams, Walker, Holmes, Todis, and Fabre (1989) to validate the social skills included in the ACCESS program for instructing social skills, this study identified the sets of social skills valued by teachers, parents, peers, and the seriously behaviorally disordered students in various school environments. The following research questions were posed:

1. Which skills identified by the Survey of Adolescent Social Skills (Williams et al., 1989) were rated as important by regular education teachers, teachers of students with behavioral disorders, regular education students, students with behavioral disorders, regular education parents, and parents of students with behavioral disorders?
2. Were there differences in the rank ordering of these skills in terms of their importance to each group?
3. What were the specific differences among the groups with regard to how they rated the specific social skill?

METHOD

Subjects

Special education directors from school districts in Washington, Iowa, and Colorado solicited volunteers from among the upper elementary and junior high (grades 4-9) teachers of the seriously behaviorally disordered in their districts. Subjects were recruited from urban, suburban, and rural schools but were not randomly selected and thus do not constitute a nonvolunteer sample. Generalizations regarding the results of this study are limited to teachers who may choose to volunteer for such tasks. The special education teachers who agreed to participate were asked to nominate a regular education teacher. The participating teachers then each nominated a student, contacted the parents of their students for consent, and distributed the surveys to parents and those students for whom they had received consent. Students who participated were from upper elementary and junior high school grades (grades 4-9).

The subject pool was comprised of a total of 383 subjects and included the following six groups: 70 regular education students (RES), 69 students with behavioral disorders (SES), 80 teachers of students with behavioral disorders (SET), 76 regular education teachers (RET), 54 parents of regular education students (REP), and 33 parents of students with behavioral disorders (SEP). Students identified as having serious behavioral disorders were so classified according to their individual states' regulations and criteria. Because state regulations and criteria vary across states, generalizations regarding the special education student data may be limited.

Instrumentation

The Adolescent Social Skills Survey (Walker et al., 1988) containing 48 items was used to collect the data. A 5-point Likert scale was provided for the subjects' use in rating the importance of each skill. The skills listed in the survey were designed to provide information regarding three behavioral domains considered to be important to adolescent adjustment.

> The identification of functional social skills—skills which will increase a child's competence in the classroom, with peers, with teachers, and with other adults—is urgently needed.

> Three behavioral domains considered important to adolescent adjustment are relating to others, adults, and self.

1. Relating to others—This domain involves skills which are needed to relate to peers, coworkers, and/or other students and to develop friendships and social support networks.
2. Relating to adults—This domain includes skills needed to relate to teachers, employers, and/or parents and to behave in ways which meet adult expectations for compliance and performance.
3. Relating to self—This domain examines those skills which allow the individual to independently and effectively manage his or her life.

There were 23 skills included in section 1 (relating to others), 9 skills in section 2 (relating to adults), and 16 skills in section 3 (relating to self). The items under each section were randomly distributed to control for item presentation or sequence effects. Three versions of the survey were generated in this manner and randomly distributed to subjects. Blank spaces were provided at the end of each section for respondents to include any additional skills they felt to be important.

Test-retest reliability had been previously reported (Timo, 1988) and ranged from .92 to .56 for all but one section. The test-retest reliability was low (.21) for special education teachers in the relating-to-others section. Williams et al. (1989) reported estimates of internal consistency (split-half reliability) for students and teachers at .96.

Procedures

Teachers, students, and parents from Washington, Colorado, and Iowa were asked to complete the survey of adolescent social skills developed by Walker and his colleagues at the University of Oregon. There were three versions of the survey, all containing identical items but arranged in differing order. Versions 1, 2, and 3 were randomly distributed to subjects. All students were given the survey after verbal instructions and asked to return them to their teachers. Any student who needed assistance in reading or interpreting an item was given the necessary help. The surveys were distributed and collected over two school years, 1987-1988 and 1988-1989.

In order to assess the importance of the skills in this survey (Research Question 1), mean scores were calculated for each group on each item (see Table 1). Spearman rank order correlations were calculated in order to assess the rank order agreement within the three adjustment domains sampled by the survey (Research Question 2). Correlations were computed using the mean scores and item rankings by section. Spearman rank order correlations were chosen because the data were ordinal and Spearman rank order correlations provided the most conservative representation of the data. In an effort to determine the specific differences among the groups regarding their opinions on specific social skills (Research Question 3), chi-square analyses were computed. Chi-square analyses were chosen because the data were ordinal (and as such did not fulfill the basic assumptions of analysis of variance). In addition, chi-square analyses allow for an examination of differences among sets of groups.

RESULTS

Question 1: Are the social skills on this survey perceived as important by teachers, students, and parents?

As 4 was defined as *Important* and 5 as *Very Important,* items with mean scores of 4.0 or above were determined to be perceived by the groups as important. Overall, teachers, students, and parents viewed the skills on this survey as important social skills. Both parent groups (REP and SEP) as well as the regular education teachers and students (RET and RES) rated at least 43 of the 48 skills (90%) as important (having a mean above 4.0) to adolescent social success.

Table 1 lists the frequency of items at various ranges of means by section. In section 1 (getting along with others) the majority of items received a score of 4.0 or higher from all six groups. However, the percentage was slightly lower for the special education students and teachers (SES and SET), each of whom rated 18 out of 23 (78%) items as important.

In section 2 (getting along with adults), the same basic pattern persists. Five of the six groups (RES, REP, SEP, RET, SET) rated all but one skill as important. All five groups indicated that the same skill—being of assistance to the teacher— was the only skill included on the list that was not critical. Students with behavioral disorders (SES) indicated that three of the nine skills were not critical to getting along with adults.

In section 3 (getting along with yourself) all of the skills were rated at 4.0 or above by all of the groups except special education teachers (SET) who rated 14 out of the 16 skills (87%) as important.

Question 2: Were there differences in the rank ordering of these skills in terms of their importance to each group?

Results are summarized in Table 2. Correlation coefficients indicated a moderate (p <.05) or high (p < .01) agreement between the parents and teachers of both special and regular education students (REP/RET, SEP/SET). The agreement level between the two student groups (RES and SES) was moderate or high (section 1 = .76, section 2 = .78, section 3 = .62). Scores from students with behavioral disorders (SES) had only moderate agreement with the adult groups (SES/RET, SES/SEP; SES/SET). Correlations for regular education students (RES) with the adult groups were somewhat higher.

Question 3: What are the specific differences among the groups regarding their opinions on specific social skills?

Section 1. Results of the chi-square analyses are summarized in Table 3. The special education students (SES) differed from the special education teachers (SET) on three items: Be Responsible, Express Anger the Right Way, and Handle Aggression. In each case, the teachers rated the skills higher. Special education students differed from regular education teachers (RET) on seven items. In each case, teachers indicated that the skills were more important. The only item in section 1 on which a significant difference occurred between the two student groups (RES, SES) was Be Considerate. Regular education students placed a higher value on this skill.

Section 2. Significant differences in the rating of the item Be of Assistance to the Teacher were observed in six of the ten group analyses. Both student groups and the parents of students with behavioral disorders indicated that Being of Assistance to the Teacher was more important than did either teacher group or the regular education parent group. The regular education teachers differed from both student groups in placing a higher value on the development of independent study skills. Special education students differed from both regular and special education teachers in placing a lesser value on Following Classroom Rules. Students with behavioral disorders also placed a lesser value on Disagreeing with Adults in an Acceptable Manner than did their parents, teachers, their

---

Regular education teachers place a high value on the development of independent study skills.

TABLE 1
List of Means Above 4.0

	SES	RES	SET	RET	SEP	REP
Section 1—Relating to others (23 items)						
4.5 - 5.0	1	2	4	6	11	5
4.25 - 4.49	2	10	7	9	7	7
4.0 - 4.24	15	10	7	6	4	7
Less than 4.0	5	1	5	2	1	4
Section 2—Relating to adults (9 items)						
4.5 - 5.0	0	1	0	2	4	2
4.25 - 4.49	0	3	6	5	4	3
4.0 - 4.24	6	4	2	1	0	3
Less than 4.0	3	1	1	1	1	1
Section 3—Relating to self (16 items)						
4.5 - 5.0	0	4	6	8	7	6
4.25 - 4.49	4	7	6	6	8	5
4.0 - 4.24	12	5	2	2	1	5
Less than 4.0	0	0	2	0	0	0

> The participants in this study viewed a majority of the social skills surveyed as important.

regular education peers, and regular education teachers.

Section 3. In this section, students with behavioral disorders differed from both teacher groups on a number of items. They (SES) differed from special education teachers on the following skills: Be Honest, Accept Consequences, and Look Good. They (SES) differed from regular education teachers on those three items and also on Have Standards for Own Behavior, Do What You Say You'll Do, and Self-Control. The special education students placed a greater emphasis on Look Good and Feel Good About Self. The teachers (SET, RET) placed greater emphasis on Have Standards for Own Behavior, Be Honest, Accept Consequences, Do What You Say You'll Do, and Self-Control. Special education students differed from their parents in that they placed a lower value on Accepting Consequences, Being Honest, and Having Standards for Own Behavior. The item Look Good was consistently more important to students than to adults.

DISCUSSION

This study was designed to examine the opinions of students, teachers, and parents regarding adolescent social skills and to understand what, if any, differences existed among the groups. Overall, the participants in this study viewed a majority of the skills surveyed as important, supporting the conclusions made by Williams et al. (1989). There were, however, some differences between

TABLE 2
Spearman Rank Correlations

Groups	REP RES	REP RET	RES RET	RES SES	RES SET	RET SES	RET SET	SEP SES	SET SES	SEP SET
Relating to others Section 1	.52 **	.91 **	.48 *	.76 **	.39 *	.40 *	.90 **	.35 *	.33	.62 **
Relating to adults Section 2	.77 *	.77 *	.47	.78 *	.48	.36	.67 *	.32	.23	.73 *
Relating to self Section 3	.65 **	.88 **	.58 *	.62 **	.60 *	.29	.82 **	.36	.17	.71 **

*$p < .05$ **$p < .01$

groups which merit discussion, especially with regard to programming for seriously behaviorally disordered students.

Students with behavioral disorders did not feel that skills such as Being of Assistance to the Teacher, Avoiding Confrontations and Problems with Adults, and Disagreeing with Adults in an Acceptable Way were as critical as other skills. This is a direct contradiction of the high value that regular and special education teachers have placed on behaviors that demonstrate compliance and cooperation, both in this study and in others reported in the literature (Cartledge et al., 1985; Kerr & Zigmond, 1986).

Regular education students rated adult-oriented skills such as Being Considerate more highly than did special education students. This difference may be the result of actual differences between the values of the two student groups. It is quite possible that the regular education students, those in the mainstream, have become proficient at fulfilling the expectations of the school system. Cairns (1986) suggests that people tend to perform their habitual responses in reoccurring situations. In this way, social systems are reinforced and maintained. Students with behavioral disorders may not feel such a part of the adult-oriented school system. As a result, they might be less interested in performing those skills valued by adults.

It is important to note that students with behavior problems may find themselves in trouble with adults for lacking the very skills that they indicated are not a priority to them. It seems quite significant that this group, alone out of the six, placed a lower value on getting along with adults. Why did the students with behavioral disorders indicate they did not place as high a value on these skills as did the other five groups? Gresham (1986) provides a conceptualization of social competency which may shed some light on this issue. He makes a distinction between skill deficits and performance deficits.

> Students with behavioral disorders may not feel a part of the adult-oriented school system.

TABLE 3
Chi Square Analyses

Group	Item	x2	Level of Significance	Rated Higher
	Section 1—Relating to others			
RES/RET	Be responsible	20.96	.00001	RET
	Aggression	13.30	.0013	RET
RES/SES	Be considerate	14.35	.0008	RES
RES/SET	Be responsible	13.35	.0013	SET
	Aggression	19.18	.0001	SET
RET/SES	Be considerate	15.88	.0004	RET
	Be responsible	30.97	.00001	RET
	Pressure	29.87	.00001	RET
	Aggression	21.85	.00001	RET
	Rejection	17.90	.0001	RET
	Ask for assistance	16.66	.0002	RET
	Listen	13.48	.0012	RET
SEP/SES	Permission	14.56	.0007	SEP
	Responsible	14.40	.0007	SEP
	Pressure	20.06	.00001	SEP
	Aggression	15.15	.0005	SEP
SET/SES	Responsible	23.81	.00001	SET
	Express	13.99	.0009	SET
	Aggression	27.54	.00001	SET
	Section 2—Relating to adults			
RES/RET	Assist teacher	17.17	.0002	RES
	Develop independent study skills	14.18	.0008	RET
RES/SET	Assist teacher	24.49	.00001	RES
RET/SES	Assist teacher	29.47	.00001	SES
	Develop independent study skills	19.99	.00001	RET
	Disagree	16.96	.0002	RET
	Follow classroom rules	17.81	.0001	RET
	Avoid confrontations	17.22	.0002	RET
SEP/SES	Develop independent study skills	12.48	.0019	SEP
SET/SES	Assist teacher	29.16	.00001	SES
	Disagree	22.48	.00001	SET
	Follow classroom rules	13.92	.0009	SET
SEP/SET	Assist teacher	24.31	.00001	SEP

Continued on next page.

TABLE 3, Continued

Group	Item	x 2	Level of Significance	Rated Higher
Section 3—Relating to self					
REP/RES	Look good	15.50	.0004	RES
RES/RET	Set goals	16.92	.0002	RET
	Look good	25.15	.00001	RES
RES/SET	Set goals	13.48	.0012	SET
	Look good	21.48	.00001	RES
RET/SES	Be honest	24.50	.00001	RET
	Have standards	15.87	.0004	RET
	Accept consequence	35.97	.00001	RET
	Look good	27.53	.00001	SES
	Do what you say	16.02	.0003	RET
	Have self-control	16.57	.0003	RET
SEP/SES	Be honest	18.26	.0001	SEP
	Accept consequence	14.25	.0008	SEP
SET/SES	Be honest	14.39	.0008	SET
	Accept consequence	31.10	.00001	SET
	Look good	24.07	.00001	SES

The basis of the distinction rests on whether or not the student knows how to perform the skill in question. Gresham (1986) posits that a lack of motivation may be one underlying cause for social skill performance deficits. If this is true, students may not be motivated to perform these skills because the rewards are not great enough or because the skills do not meet their needs.

The issue of social significance should play a major part in the design and implementation of behavioral interventions. The social significance of a particular skill is usually based on the subjective judgments of relevant others in the students' environment (Gresham, 1986; Kazdin, 1977). Responses from teachers in this study have indicated that certain skills are necessary for success, at least in the academic environment. It becomes imperative, then, to understand why students with behavioral disorders do not value and perform these skills. The answer to such fundamental questions might determine how one approaches these skills in a training program. One caution, however, must be raised. Since the reported reliability of special education teachers was low, further investigations regarding their perceptions should be conducted.

As expected, both teacher groups placed the greatest importance on those skills that would aid in the smooth running of the classroom. Both teacher groups focused on compliance skills such as accepting consequences and following directions as major requirements for their students. Independent study skills and following classroom rules without undue supervision were also valued by both teacher groups. These responses are consistent with other

> The issue of social significance should play a major part in the design and implementation of behavioral interventions.

> It could be very important for teachers of students with behavioral disorders to encourage their students to start to develop standards for their behavior that reflect those of general education students.

research which has indicated that teachers place the highest value on adaptive behaviors that ensure a smooth running classroom (Calkins et al., 1984; Cartledge et al., 1985; Walker, 1984; Walker & Rankin, 1983).

There were, however, differences between the two groups of teachers. For example, special education teachers placed greater emphasis on Expressing Anger the Right Way and on Disagreeing with Adults in an Acceptable Way than did regular education teachers. This difference may reflect the different populations that they serve.

Regular education teachers also felt it was important for students to have standards for their own behavior. It could be very important for teachers of students with behavioral disorders to encourage their students to start to develop standards for their behavior that reflect those of general education students. It also seems imperative that they develop a set of independent behaviors that will enable them to plan their activities and monitor their progress and behavior. The work of Lloyd and his colleagues (1989) in the area of self-management offers several suggestions for planners of social skills programs.

Another interesting finding of this study is the lack of concordance of the values expressed by the children with behavioral disorders and all other groups. With a data set that is so similar across groups, the lack of correlation between the findings for this group and the others is noteworthy. A review of Table 2 shows that a majority of their ratings are discordant with the other groups studied. This is especially true in section 2, relating to adults. A functional approach to analyzing behavior suggests that chains of behavior produce an effect (Neel, 1984). The success or failure does not depend on its acceptance by others, but its ability to produce a desired result. Using this framework, social skills are viewed as a set of (or series of) behaviors required to achieve a social goal in a particular situation (Neel, Meadows, & Scott, 1990). If we were to assume a functional approach to analyzing social skills, it would seem that a major component in the training of social skills would have to be teaching children with behavioral disorders to value interacting with adults. This may require a restructuring of the methods for delivering services that we now use (Neel & Cessna, 1990; Neel, Cessna, Swize, & Borock, 1988).

If one of the major goals of a social skills training program is to prepare students for reentry into the general education classroom, then it seems critical to examine the priorities of the teachers of those classrooms, who have shown themselves to be highly oppositional to the behavior of many mainstreamed children (Sarason & Doris, 1978). The perception of general education teachers is an important one. When teachers design programs to teach children with behavioral disorders those skills required to integrate effectively into general education environments, they should be aware of the skills which are highly valued by regular education teachers and students.

It is also not surprising that students prefer immediate social goals to those with more long-term indirect payoffs. In fact, the degree to which students and teachers agree might be considered a measure of socialization toward adult values. Again as expected, the ratings of general education students on social skill items correspond more closely to the adults than did the ratings of children with behavioral disorders. These findings, though not unexpected, do accent the need for inclusion of training of skills required by youth to become successful with their peers and adults.

The data in this study, however, also show that there is another set of skills that are critical to the social success of children with behavioral disorders: those that effect short-term peer adjustment. In fact, these latter skills have a greater value for students than those most valued by their teachers or parents. The need to develop effective training programs to address these skills can no longer be ignored. If school programs are going to be able to meet the needs of all their students, they will have to realign their priorities to include peer focused social skills training (Neel, Cessna et al., 1988).

CONCLUSION

The results of this study indicate that parents, students, and teachers viewed the 48 skills on this survey as important. However, it must be remembered that the participants in this study were subjected to a *forced choice* condition. They were provided a prechosen list of skills and asked to rate their importance. This limits the degree to which the data may be generalized. While it is true that this study and others like it (Timo, 1988; Williams et al., 1989) have shown these skills to be important, they have not proven them to be critical. Subjects in this study were only asked to react to a fixed set of skills. Having groups of people generate their own lists of skills may produce different skills. Further research needs to be done that will determine which of these skills are critical to successful integration.

Despite the possibly limiting effects mentioned above, understanding the differences among the groups in this study will begin to increase understanding of why social skills training programs do not work as well as expected. If it is true that many of the social skills included in training programs were chosen on the basis of face validity (Kazdin & Matson, 1981), then this kind of empirical testing is one way to understand which skills will be valued and reinforced. Skills that are not considered valuable by students, and those who work and live with them, have less chance of becoming a functional part of the student's behavior (McConnell, 1987).

Because the goal of many social skills training programs is to have the students return to the mainstream classroom, the differences between regular education teachers and special education students should be considered carefully. More significant differences occurred between these two groups than any other possible combination. In order for students, especially students with behavioral disorders, to benefit from social skills training programs, the skills they learn must be important to them and to the many other people with whom they interact. Students and adults need to be aware of their own and each other's values. This study is just a beginning in the effort to understand which skills are critical and why.

Future research needs to be directed towards developing a functionally valid list of critical social skills. It seems quite possible that if this many differences exist under a forced choice condition, even more differences in values and priorities might be revealed under different experimental conditions. It is essential that future training programs include skills that will make functional differences in students' behavior and in the judgments of those who come in contact with them.

REFERENCES

Asher, S. R., & Hymel, S. (1981). Children's social competence in peer relations: Sociometric and behavioral

> Future research needs to be directed toward developing a functionally valid list of critical social skills.

assessment. In J. D. Wine & M. D. Syme (Eds.), *Social competence* (pp. 125-157). New York: Guilford Press.

Asher, S. R., & Taylor, A. R. (1983). Social skill training with children: Evaluating processes and outcomes. *Studies in Educational Evaluation, 8,* 237-245.

Bellack, A. S. (1983). Recurrent problems in the behavioral assessment of social skill. *Behavioral Research Therapy, 21(l),* 29-41.

Bruininks, V. L. (1978). Actual and perceived peer status of learning disabled students in mainstream programs. *Journal of Special Education, 12,* 51-58.

Cairns, R. B. (1986). A contemporary perspective on social development. In P. S. Strain, M. J. Guralnick, & H. M. Walker (Eds.), *Children's social behavior: Development assessment and modification* (pp. 3-47). Orlando, FL: Academic Press.

Calkins, C. F., Walker, H. M., Bacon-Prue, A., Gibson, B. A., Martinson, M., Offner, R., & Intagliata, J. (1984). *The learning and adjustment process.* Kansas City: University of Missouri, Institute for Human Development.

Cartledge, G., Frew, T, & Zaharias, J. (1985). Social skill needs of mainstreamed students: Peer and teacher perceptions. *Learning Disabilities Quarterly, 8, 132-139.*

Combs, M. L., & Slaby, D. A. (1977). Social skills training with children. In B. B. Lahey & A. E. Kazdin *(Eds.), Advances in child clinical psychology (Vol* 1, pp. 39-60). New York: Plenum.

Gottman, J., Gonso, J., & Schuler, P. (1976). Teaching social skills to isolated children. *Journal of Abnormal Psychology, 4, 179-197.*

Gresham, F. M. (1981). Social skills training with handicapped children: A review. *Review of Educational Research, 51(l),139-176.*

Gresham, F. M. (1982). Misguided mainstreaming: The case for social skills training with handicapped children. *Exceptional Children, 49,* 49-54.

Gresham, F. M. (1986). Conceptual issues in the assessment of social competence in children. In P.S. Strain, M. J. Guralnick, & H. M. Walker (Eds.), *Children's social behavior: Development, assessment, and modification* (pp. 143-179). Orlando, FL: Academic Press.

Gronlund, H., & Anderson, L. (1962). Personality characteristics of socially accepted, socially neglected, and socially rejected junior high school pupils. In J. Sedeman (Ed.), *Educating for mental health* (pp. 162-173). New York: Cromwell.

Kauffman, J. M. (1989). *Characteristics of behavior disorders of children and youth* (4th ed.).Columbus, OH: Merrill.

Kazdin, A. E. (1 977). Assessing the clinical or applied importance of behavior change through social validation. *Behavior Modification, 1,* 427-452.

Kazdin, A. E., & Matson, J. L. (1981). Social validation in mental retardation. *Applied Research in Mental Retardation, 2,* 39-53.

Kerr, M., & Zigmond, N. (1986). What do high school teachers want? A study of expectations and standards. *Education and Treatment of Children, 9,* 239-249.

Knold, J. A. (Ed.). (1985). *Employee training needs as expressed by employers in Washington state.* Olympia: Washington State Commission for Vocational Education.

LeCroy, C. W. (1983). Social skills training with adolescents: A review. *Child and Youth Services, 5,* 91-116.

Lloyd, J. W., Landrum, T J., & Hallahan, D. P. (1989). *Self-monitoring applications for classroom intervention* (Virginia Behavior Disorders Project, Research Report No. 8). Charlottesville: University of Virginia.

McConnell, S. R. (1987). Entrapment effects and the generalization and maintenance of social skills training for elementary school students with behavioral disorders. *Behavioral Disorders, 12,* 252-263.

Michelson, L., & Wood, R. (1980). Behavioral assessment and training of children's social skills. *Progress in Behavior Modification, 9,* 241-291.

Morgan, S. R. (1977). A descriptive analysis of maladjusted behavior in socially rejected children. *Behavioral Disorders, 3,* 23-30.

Neel, R. S. (1984). Teaching social routines to behaviorally disordered youth. In C. R. Smith & E. McGinnis (Eds.), *Educational instruments in behavioral disorders* (pp. 73-88). Des Moines: Iowa State Department of Education.

Neel, R. S., & Cessna, K. K. (1990). *Do these behaviors make sense?* Manuscript submitted for publication.

Neel, R. S., Cessna, K., Swize, M., & Borock, J. (1988). *Position paper on serving S.I.E.B.D. students.* Unpublished manuscript, Colorado State Department of Education, Denver.

Neel, R. S., Meadows, N. B., Levine, P., & Edgar, E. B. (1988). What happens after special education: A statewide follow-up study of secondary students who have behavioral disorders. *Behavioral Disorders, 13,* 209-216.

Neel, R. S., Meadows, N. B., & Scott, C. M. (1990*). Determining social tasks: A preliminary report.* Manuscript submitted for publication.

Roff, M. (1970). Childhood social interactions and young adult bad conduct. *Journal of Abnormal and Social Psychology, 63,* 333-337.

Roff, M., Sells, B., & Golden, M. (1972*). Social adjustment and personality development in children.* Minneapolis: University of Minnesota Press.

Sabornie, E. J. (1985). Social mainstreaming of handicapped students: Facing an unpleasant reality. *Remedial and Special Education, 6(2), 12-16.*

Sarason, S., & Doris, J. (1978). Mainstreaming: Dilemmas, opposition, opportunities. In M. Reynolds (Ed.), *Futures of education for exceptional children: Emerging structures* (pp. 3-39). Reston, VA: The Council for Exceptional Children.

Schloss, P. J., Schloss, C. N., Wood, C. E., & Kiehl, W. S. (1986). A critical review of social skills research with behaviorally disordered students. *Behavioral Disorders, 12,* 1-14.

Sheperd, G. (1980). The treatment of social difficulties in special environments. In P. Feldman & J. Orford (Eds.), *Psychological problems: The social context* (pp. 312-359). New York: John Wiley & Sons.

Stengel, E. (1971). *Suicide and attempted suicide.* Middlesex, NJ: Penguin.

Timo, K. S. (1988). *Adolescent social skills validation by teachers and students.* Unpublished master's thesis, University of Washington, Seattle.

Ullman, C. A. (1957). Teacher, peers, and tests as predictors of adjustment. *Journal of Educational Psychology, 48,* 257-267.

Walker, H. M. (1984). The social behavior survival program (SBS): A systematic approach to the integration of handicapped children into less restrictive settings. *Education and Treatment of Children, 6,* 421-441.

Walker, H. M., & Rankin, R. (1983). Assessing the behavioral expectations and demands of less restrictive settings. *School Psychology Review, 12,* 274-284.

Walker, H. M., Todis, B., Holmes, D., & Horton, G. (1988). *The Walker social skills curriculum.* Austin, TX: Pro-Ed.

Williams, S. L., Walker, H. M., Holmes, D., Todis, B., & Fabre, T. R. (1989). Social validation of adolescent social skills by teacher and students. *Remedial and Special Education, 10(4),* 18-27.

Social Interaction Research and Families of Behaviorally Disordered Children: A Critical Review and Forward Look

James Fox
Sarah Savelle

ABSTRACT: *This article critically reviews research on the social interactions of behaviorally disordered children with family members. Behaviorally disordered children are in part characterized by their difficulty in establishing or maintaining positive social relationships. This includes conduct disordered, socially withdrawn, and autistic children. Most applied research on social development has been conducted in educational settings. Yet, parents and siblings are typically acknowledged as the earliest and one of the most enduring influences on children's social development. Descriptive and intervention research that includes direct observational measures of social interaction between behaviorally disordered children, their siblings, or parents are reviewed. Two principal questions are addressed: (a) to what degree have these research studies shown that behaviorally disordered children exhibit deficits in positive interaction with family members when compared to nonhandicapped children and their families; and (b) what interventions have been shown to be effective in increasing positive interaction between behaviorally disordered children and their families? Issues and questions for future research in this area are discussed.*

Difficulty in establishing and maintaining social relationships is one of the defining characteristics of behaviorally disordered children and youth (Bower & Lambert, 1961; Kauffman, 1985). Such problems in social development include conduct disorders in which the child typically engages in negative interactions with other children and adults, and social withdrawal in which the child either fails to engage in or actively avoids interaction with others (Michaelson & Mannario, 1986).

Over the past 50 years applied researchers have sought to (a) describe more precisely the nature, course, and implications of disorders in social behavior; and (b) develop and empirically evaluate intervention procedures with which to teach more adaptive social skills and increase positive interaction. In many respects our understanding of these problems and our intervention technology have improved substantially (Hops, 1982; Strain, 1983; Strain & Fox, 1981; Strain, Guralnick, & Walker, 1986; Van Hasselt, Hersen, Whitehill, & Bellack, 1979).

> The bulk of social interaction research has focused on peer relations in educational settings.

However, the bulk of social interaction research has focused on peer relations in educational settings (Day, Fox, Shores, Lindeman, & Stowitschek, 1983; Foster & Ritchey, 1979; Fox, Day, & McEvoy, in press; Powell, Salzberg, Rule, Levy, & Itzkowitz, 1983). With the exception of conduct disordered children (e.g., Patterson, 1982), rarely have investigators subjected parent and sibling interactions to direct analysis or evaluated their relationship to the development of peer-related social skills and interaction. This seems a particularly glaring omission for two reasons. Parents and siblings have been conceptualized as the earliest and potentially one of the most enduring socialization influences (Hartup, 1970, 1983; Maccoby & Martin, 1983). Secondly, naturalistic research with normally developing children indicates that nuclear family members can and do play an active role in the shaping of a child's *social* repertoire (e.g., Abramovitch, Corter, Pepler, & Stanhope, 1986; Dunn & Kendrick, 1982; Lamb, 1978); the few existing studies with handicapped children suggest a similar role for those families (James & Egel, 1986; Powell et al., 1983).

Our purpose in writing this article is twofold: (a) to critically review social interaction research with behaviorally disordered children, their siblings, and parents; and (b) to suggest areas for future research. In particular this review will address research in regard to two questions:

1. Do behaviorally disordered children exhibit deficits in social interaction with parents and/or siblings when contrasted with families of nonhandicapped children?

2. How can positive interaction between behaviorally disordered children and family members be increased?

By social interaction we refer to behaviors directed by one person to another, the purpose or function of which is to initiate and maintain the exchange of behaviors between the two interactants. We will not emphasize studies of social exchanges between a child and other family members which are primarily managerial (commands, compliance, etc.) or tutorial—those in which one family member attempts to teach the other certain academic, cognitive, or self-help skills. This is not to deny the importance of such behavioral exchanges or their possible relevance to social interaction between behaviorally disordered children and their families. Rather, it is primarily a practical distinction. Such studies have not typically addressed social interaction as we have defined it here. In addition, reviews of the use of behavior management procedures by parents with their emotionally disturbed children are available elsewhere (e.g., Gordon & Davidson, 1981).

Descriptive Analysis of Family Interaction

Home-based, observational analyses of normally developing children's interactions with family members have increased considerably in recent years (e.g., Abramovitch et al., 1986; Brody, Stoneman, & MacKinnon, 1982; Dunn & Kendrick, 1982; Lamb, 1978; Stoneman, Brody, & MacKinnon, 1984). Analyses of the family interactions of behaviorally disordered children under naturalistic conditions have a somewhat more sporadic history.

Behavior problem/conduct disordered children. Outcomes of family-based observational studies have been virtually unanimous in distinguishing conduct disordered and nonreferred children in terms of their inappropriate behaviors and have also found that their parents and siblings are characterized by greater levels of negative social behaviors than in families of nonreferred children (Arnold, Levine, & Patterson, 1975; Horne, 1980, as cited in Patterson, 1982; Patterson, 1976, 1982; Snyder, 1977; Taplin & Reid, 1977). However, differences in positive interactions between family members have been less clearly established.

Two studies have reported differences in positive social behaviors between conduct disordered and nonreferred children. Bernal and her colleagues (Bernal, Delfini, North, & Kreutzer, 1976; Delfini, Bernal, & Rosen, 1976) observed two groups of young boys—a discipline problem group referred for fighting, disobeying, arguing, and so forth, and a normal (nonreferred) group from regular kindergarten and first grade classes. Four 30-min observations were conducted for each child. The home data indicated that problem boys exhibited significantly more annoying and deviant behavior and significantly fewer desirable (e.g., on-task, appropriate verbal and nonverbal interaction) and compliant behaviors than nonproblem boys. However, the absolute difference in rate of desirable behavior was rather small, the most pronounced differences between the two groups being in terms of annoying and deviant behaviors. Also, it was not clear from the data analyses to whom, parent or sibling, these desirable social behaviors were directed nor were specific responses to these behaviors reported.

Later, Mash and Mercer (1979) compared deviant (clinically referred) and nondeviant (nonreferred) boys under two conditions—playing alone and with their brothers—in a laboratory playroom. Deviance was defined in terms of clinical referral status (aggression, noncompliance, and disturbed peer relations) and scores on the *Walker Problem*

Behavior Identification Checklist. Normal subjects were volunteers from local community groups and schools. During the sibling condition, normal subjects and their siblings engaged in significantly more cooperative play whereas deviant subjects engaged in more negative verbal and physical interactions. Also, for normal sibling pairs both their interactive behaviors appeared to be more reciprocal than those of deviant sibling pairs. However, the most frequent behavior for both groups during the sibling condition was *solitary* play.

The findings from Patterson's (1976) study of clinically referred, aggressive boys and nonreferred boys stand in contrast to those of the preceding studies. In-home observations were conducted using a multicategory observation system (Patterson, Ray, Shaw, & Cobb, 1969) designed to assess both positive and negative behaviors. Although rates of eight deviant behaviors (negative commands, disapproval, humiliate, ignore, noncomply, negativism, tease, and yell) were significantly higher for aggressive subjects, none of the comparisons for prosocial behavior rates were significantly different. However, these comparisons were based on total rates and did not indicate to whom the person being observed directed these behaviors.

It does appear that the social exchanges of conduct disordered children and their family members are less reciprocal. Analyses of naturally contingencies provided by family members of conduct disordered boys referred for treatment were reported by Taplin and Reid (1977). Baseline data indicated that parents were about as likely to positively consequate deviant behavior as they were prosocial behavior. Snyder (1977) examined interactional differences between problem and nonproblem *families* with a male child between 5 and 10

> Outcomes of family-based observational studies have been virtually unanimous in distinguishing conduct disordered and nonreferred children in terms of their inappropriate behaviors and have also found that their parents and siblings are characterized by greater levels of negative social behaviors than in families of nonreferred children.

> Some studies have indicated that conduct disordered children engage in fewer positive social behaviors with family members than do normal children while others have not found any significant differences in the rate of prosocial behaviors between conduct disordered and nonreferred children.

years old. Groups were defined by the child's score on the *Behavior Problem Checklist* and parents' reports of marital conflict on the *Locke-Wallace Marital Adjustment Scale*. Families were videotaped once for 45 minutes in a laboratory room arranged as living room-play room combination. For data analyses, observational categories were reduced to one of two classes—pleasing and displeasing behavior—using families' averaged ratings of each category. Responses were reduced to one of three contingencies—positive, negative, or neutral.

Although most behavior in both types of families was pleasing, the rate of displeasing behavior in problem families was approximately twice that of nonproblem families. (Analyses of differences in pleasing behavior rates were not reported.) Further, problem family members provided significantly fewer positive and more neutral or aversive consequences for pleasing behaviors; they also received fewer aversive and more positive consequences for displeasing behavior. Finally, conditional probability analyses indicated that problem family members were significantly less likely than nonproblem family members to repeat pleasing behaviors that were followed by positive consequences and more likely to continue displeasing behaviors followed by aversive consequences.

To summarize briefly, some studies have indicated that conduct disordered children engage in fewer positive social behaviors with family members than do normal children (Dellfini et al., 1976; Mash & Mercer, 1979) while others have not found any significant differences in the rate of prosocial behaviors (Patterson, 1976) between conduct disordered and nonreferred children. The disparity in these findings may result from methodological differences between the studies, including the selection criteria for conduct disordered subjects, differences in behavior definitions, conditions of observation and observational procedures, and the units of analyses. For example, some investigators (Patterson, 1976, 1980; Taplin & Reid, 1977) have selected conduct disordered subjects primarily on the basis of their referral to a treatment program due to problems characterizing conduct disordered children (aggression, noncompliance, tantrums, etc.) whereas other researchers used additional criteria such as subjects' scores on a standardized behavior checklist (Mass & Mercer, 1979). Snyder (1977), in fact, selected problem families using a combination of child referral status *and* behavior checklist scores, and parents' scores on a marital adjustment scale.

Then, too, some studies have used interval recording procedures (Bernal et al., 1976; Delfini et al., 1976; Mash & Mercer, 1979) while other studies have used continuous, sequential recording (Patterson, 1976, 1980; Snyder, 1977). Continuous sequential recording should be more sensitive to differences in the frequency/rate of behavior, yet studies employing less precise interval recording have reported differences in conduct disordered and normal children's social interactions with family members. Studies have also varied in terms of the physical location and setting conditions (home based vs. laboratory analog) in which observations have been conducted. Until these and other procedural/methodological variations between studies are controlled or systematically investigated, comparisons across studies will remain tenuous.

Children exhibiting social withdrawal. The term *social withdrawal* refers to a low rate or avoidance of social interaction (Strain & Fox, 1981). Used in this way, it refers to a general behavioral deficit that may be exhibited by a diverse array of children, including those who are otherwise normally developing as well as children with more pervasive handicaps (e.g., autism, mental retardation). Hereafter, we will refer to these otherwise normally-developing children as "withdrawn children."

In an earlier review of social withdrawal, Finch and Hops (1983) briefly described a study of 30 intact families. Preliminary analyses were said to indicate that:

> Parents of withdrawn children showed somewhat reduced rates of prosocial behavior compared to parents of either the high average or highly sociable children. In addition, fathers of the low sociability children provided more adverse and fewer prosocial consequences for child prosocial behavior than fathers of the other two groups.

To date, this is the only reference to an observational analysis comparing the family interactions of withdrawn and nonwithdrawn children of which we are aware.

Social withdrawal has been one of the defining characteristics of autism since the disorder was first described by Kanner (1943). Indeed, as Schopler and Mesibov (1986) have noted, some consider social deficits to be the basic problem of autism, and as DeMyer (1979) noted in her interview studies with parents, some of their most painful experiences and difficult decisions center upon the autistic child's reactions to people and their social distance. Yet, home-based observational studies of autistic children have been and continue to be extremely rare, this despite the fact that clinical and parent reports suggest some autistic individuals make at least some social adaptations and interact more appropriately as they age (DeMyer, 1979; Kanner, 1971; Kanner, Rodriguez, & Ashenden, 1972).

Possibly the earliest home-based observation analysis of an autistic child was reported by Lichstein and Wahler (1976). A 5-year-old autistic boy was observed both at home with his family (parents and nonhandicapped older sister) and in two classroom settings. A total of 75 30-min observations were obtained in the home and 42 in each school setting. The subject's behavior was scored in terms of various social, nonsocial, and autistic behavior categories (Wahler, House, & Stambaugh, 1976). Over the course of the study both social and nonsocial behaviors varied considerably. In the home, the subject engaged in little interaction with his sister, rarely initiated interactions with any family member, and on the average, interacted infrequently with his parents (approximately 11% of the time). The most frequent behaviors at home were nonsocial, autistic behaviors such as self-stimulation and noninteraction. Finally, the investigators also noted that the boy rarely engaged in any sustained toy play either alone or with others.

Martin and Graunke (1979) assessed the home behavior of 15 autistic children and adolescents 5 to 13 years old. Using Patterson, Ray, Shaw, and Cobb's (1969) observation system, subjects were observed for 45 minutes on 5 different occasions—4 weekdays and 1 weekend day. Individual behaviors were subsumed under three general categories— deviant, nondeviant, and prosocial. As a group the autistic subjects engaged in relatively little deviant behavior (e.g., self-destructive, self-stimulation). Nondeviant behaviors (verbal neutral, physical contact, independent activity) were most frequent, accounting for approximately 60% of the subjects' behavior. Prosocial behaviors (e.g., compliance, laugh, physical positive, play) were intermediate in occurrence, accounting for approximately 34% of subjects' behavior. However, consid-

---

Social withdrawal has been one of the defining characteristics of autism.

> Compared to nondisabled children, children with mental retardation appear deficient not in the overall amount of interaction with family members but in certain aspects of interaction.

erable intersubject variability was noted in all classes of behavior. Although all family members were more likely to respond positively than negatively to the autistic subjects, siblings were less likely to respond positively to deviant behaviors than were parents.

Donnellan, Anderson, and Mesaros (1984) conducted observations of 7 autistic boys ranging in age from 2½ to 11 years. Autistic child-family member interactions were videotaped once during each of three typical home activities—mealtime, free time, and transition time (arriving home from school). These tapes were scored using a rating system designed to assess "family-member interactions, stereotypy, and environmental variables that might have influenced them." However, length of the observation sessions and the specific codes were not described in the report. Subject children interacted with families during approximately 56% of the intervals. Interactions were more likely to occur during intervals in which there was little or no stereotypy rather than during longer bouts of stereotypy. Stereotypic behavior occurred 19% of the time and was particularly prevalent during unstructured activities.

Studies of the family interactions of mentally retarded children have been conducted somewhat more frequently. These studies suggest that we proceed with conceptual and methodological caution in attempting to descriptively analyze family interactions. Studies of both parent-child (Eheart, 1982; Stoneman, Brody, & Abbott, 1983; Terdal, Jackson, & Garner, 1976) and child-sibling social interactions (Stoneman & Brody, in press; Stoneman, Brody, Davis, & Crapps, 1986) indicate that the interactional differences between mentally retarded and normally developing children may not always be apparent as a deficit in the overall amount of interaction. Rather, differences between handicapped and nonhandicapped children's family interactions appear to have more to do with particular types of social encounters.

For example, compared with normally developing children, mentally retarded children are less responsive to parents' (Eheart, 1982; Stoneman et al., 1983; Terdal et al., 1976) and siblings' (Stoneman & Brody, in press) social overtures. Their parents and siblings are more likely to engage them in directive/managerial/teaching interactions. Also, Stoneman et al. (1986) found that nonhandicapped siblings were more likely to engage in solitary play during several activities than were sibling dyads with a mentally retarded child. In a recent home-based observational study, we too found that as a group not only did mentally retarded children engage in less solitary play (and more unoccupied behavior), they also received and emitted higher total rates of positive initiations and interactions with both their siblings and mothers (Savelle, Fox, & Phillips, 1987). Thus, compared to nonhandicapped children, mentally retarded children appear deficient not in the overall amount of interaction with family members but in certain aspects of interaction (i.e., less responsive to others and fewer playful interactions).

In summary, there have been very few studies of the in-home family interactions of either withdrawn (Finch & Hops, 1983) or of autistic children (Donnellan et al., 1984; Lichstein & Wahler, 1976; Martin & Graunke, 1979). Our knowledge of withdrawn children's interactions with parents and siblings, though considered vital to socialization (Hartup, 1983; Maccoby & Martin, 1983), is seriously lacking empirically-based description. Social withdrawal has been considered a clinically significant problem at least since the turn of the century (Campbell, 1986) and is a ubiquitous factor in the study of children's behavioral disorders (Kauffman, 1985; Quay, 1979). Yet even today we can say little about the quantity or quality of withdrawn children's interactions, positive or negative, with family members.

The situation is little better when we consider autistic children. To date the several studies (Donnellan et al., 1984; Lichstein & Wahler, 1976; Martin & Graunke, 1979) have produced what would appear to be considerably different estimates of positive social interaction between autistic children and their families. In addition, these studies have yielded disparate findings regarding stereotypic/other aberrant responses. Lichstein and Wahler (1976) found this to be the most predominant behavior in their analyses, but Martin and Graunke (1979) and Donnellan et al. (1984) found stereotypy to be comparatively infrequent in their group analyses. The implications of differing rates of stereotypy were indicated by the Donnellan study which found, not altogether surprisingly, that interactions were unlikely to occur during periods of stereotypy. Lichstein and Wahler (1976), in an intensive single subject analysis, found a stable, inverse correlation between their categories of "self-stimulation" and "nonaversive adult social attention." These results suggest that it is important to consider the occurrence and perhaps influence of aberrant behavior on the social relations of autistic children and their families. For example, stereotypic behavior may function to permit the autistic child to escape or avoid interaction with others.

As with studies of conduct disordered children, attempts to synthesize or draw conclusions from the few analyses of autistic children are further complicated by methodological and procedural differences (e.g., behavior categories, observational procedures, length and frequency of observations, setting conditions, individual vs. group analyses) between studies. To some degree, the "different" outcomes may be more apparent than real. Clinical and anecdotal reports indicate that at least some autistic persons become more social as they age (see DeMyer, 1979; Kanner, 1971; Kanner et al., 1972). Thus, one might expect different results given the comparatively young age of Lichstein and Wahler's (1976) subject and the substantial age ranges of the children in the Martin and Graunke (1979) and the Donnellan et al. (1984) studies.

The differing results may also have been due to the differing analytic approaches taken by the several investigators, intensive single case (Lichstein & Wahler, 1976), and group statistical analysis (Donnellan et al., 1984; Martin & Graunke, 1979). Given the substantial intersubject and intrasubject variability in social behaviors reported by Martin and Graunke (1979) and Lichstein and Wahler (1976), respectively, it is not at all surprising that three such discrepant estimates of interaction could result.

At the same time, however, it may be that—like mentally retarded children—behaviorally disordered children cannot be reliably distinguished from their nonhandicapped counterparts in terms of the overall amount of interaction with parents or siblings. Autistic and mentally retarded children sometimes exhibit similar behavior deficits and excesses, and thus it may be that the bulk of autistic children's interactions with family members are, as those of mentally retarded children, composed of directive, teaching, or managerial social exchanges. To address this possibility, it will be necessary to employ more fine-grained behavior categories and analyses than those reported to date.

> It may be that—like children with mental retardation—children with behavioral disorders cannot be reliably distinguished from their nondisabled counterparts in terms of the overall amount of interaction with parents or siblings.

> There have been relatively few observational studies of the in-home, family interaction patterns of children with behavioral disorders.

General summary and conclusions—descriptive analysis of family interaction. In summary, there have been relatively few observational studies of the in-home, family interaction patterns of behaviorally disordered children. This lack of research is particularly acute for withdrawn and autistic children. Second, the extant research studies do not clearly delineate the degree to which different types of behaviorally disordered children (conduct disordered, withdrawn, autistic) are characterized by deficits in positive social interaction with parents or siblings when compared to normally developing children. Third—and possibly related to the second point—in each of the populations reviewed here, methodological and procedural differences between studies further delimit the conclusions that can be drawn.

A number of issues, both substantive and methodological, confront those interested in pursuing descriptive analyses of behaviorally disordered children's family interactions. In view of the dearth of studies in this area and the sometimes conflicting, variable results of existing studies, there is an obvious need for further research. However, we think it unlikely that simply increasing the number of descriptive studies will, by itself, advance our understanding of the nature and extent of family interactions.

Rather, future investigators would do well to heed the advice offered 20 years ago by Bijou, Peterson, and Ault (1968) regarding precise descriptions if not direct control of setting conditions in a descriptive study. Many of the studies we reviewed have attempted to provide an account of the "natural" amount of interaction, imposing a minimum of restrictions. Yet, these "natural conditions" of observation have varied both within and between studies. We have argued that variations in physical and social setting factors may very well have imposed variability in subjects' interactive behavior within and between studies.

For example, Patterson and his colleagues (Arnold et al., 1975; Patterson, 1976; Taplin & Reid, 1977) required that all family members be present and that they restrict themselves to certain rooms of the house during observation; Mash and Mercer (1979) and Snyder (1977), however, restricted their observations to interactions between subjects and certain family members (siblings and parents, respectively) and conducted their observations in contrived settings. Research with normally developing children has shown that the type and frequency of their social interactions vary as a function of changes in the social composition of a setting (Brody, Stoneman, & MacKinnon, 1982; Corter, Abramovitch, & Pepler, 1983). What is needed, then, are studies that provide quantitative descriptions of behaviorally disordered children's family interactions in the context of specifically defined and measured setting conditions. Such a database would likely allow us to make more informed judgments about the need for and nature of social behavior interventions.

A third issue is the conceptualization and measurement of social behaviors in family interaction research. The continued use of global categories such as *positive, prosocial,* or *pleasing* interaction will not permit us to identify the specific skills which are critical to and facilitative of positive social exchanges between family members. Indeed, if we take an interactionist reciprocal social exchange perspective on children's social development (see Shores' article in this issue), then it becomes imperative to more specifically analyze and describe the components of effective social interaction. Such an approach has proven fruitful in school-based studies (Strain, 1983;

Tremblay, Strain, Hendrickson, & Shores, 1981) and in home-based studies of nonhandicapped (Abramovitch et al., 1986), mentally retarded (Stoneman & Brady, in press), and conduct disordered children (Patterson, 1982). Combined with the contextual or setting factor analyses this reciprocal perspective should permit the development of a more useful descriptive database.

Family-based Intervention Research

Conduct disordered children. In one of the earliest reports of home-based behavioral treatment, Hawkins, Peterson, Schweid, and Bijou (1966) described the parent-mediated treatment of a young boy exhibiting tantrums, disobedience, and aggression to objects and people, especially his younger sister. These "objectionable behaviors" were observed and then treated by having the mother apply timeout contingent upon their occurrence and "occasionally" attend positively to the subject's appropriate play. Objectionable behaviors decreased during this intervention. Although never systematically recorded, positive interactions between mother and child reportedly increased also.

O'Leary, O'Leary, and Becker (1967) dealt more directly with increasing positive interaction between a 6-year-old behaviorally disordered boy and his younger brother. Cooperative, deviant, and isolate play were observed in the home. Prior to intervention, the boys' play interactions were characterized by fighting, breaking toys and furniture, tantrums, and noncompliance to parents' instructions. Differential reinforcement of cooperative play and timeout for deviant behavior were applied first by the experimenters and later by the parents. The intervention procedures reliably increased cooperative play between the siblings. Interestingly, isolate play also increased during intervention.

Leitenberg, Burchard, Burchard, Fuller, and Lysaght (1977) contrasted the effects of two differential attention procedures designed to reduce sibling conflict between 6 behavior problem children and their siblings. Sibling conflict (verbal and physical aggression) and appropriate interaction (playing games together, sharing, helping, conversation) were observed in the home. Following baseline, parents applied two different interventions in alternating weeks. Differential reinforcement of other behavior (DRO) involved parents delivering contingent praise and pennies to both children for each minute in which sibling conflict did not occur. The second procedure, reinforcement of appropriate interaction (RAI), consisted of the same rewards delivered only after an interval in which the siblings had interacted appropriately. Both DRO and RAI reduced sibling conflict equivalently and both were associated with increases in appropriate interaction. However, RAI resulted in substantially more appropriate sibling interaction.

Lavigueur (1976) evaluated a slightly different approach to increasing siblings' positive interactions in which siblings as well as parents served as intervention agents. Subjects were two disruptive children from two different families and their siblings, neither of whom were behavior problems. Interval recording sampled positive and negative verbalizations, offering and giving help, aggression, noncompliance, playing, and positive affect. Following baseline, two procedures were contrasted in sequential phases: (a) parent application of differential attention and timeout contingent upon the occurrence of target behaviors; and (b) application of differential attention by both parents and siblings. Initial targets were positive and negative verbalizations. Later, "offering help" and "giving help" were added for families A and B,

Family-based intervention research is critical to the field.

> Differential reinforcement of prosocial behavior and reductive contingencies for inappropriate behavior have not always increased positive interaction in families of children with conduct disorders.

respectively. In family A, positive verbalizations and offering help increased after the parent-only intervention but were not further affected by the combined parent-sibling intervention. However, negative verbalizations did not decrease until the combined interventions were applied. In family B, all three behavior targets were changed by the parent intervention alone. During the last two phases of parent and parent-sibling intervention, play between the siblings (never a direct treatment target) also increased.

Thus, although increases were obtained in several categories of positive interaction, the sibling intervention effects were minimal.

Differential reinforcement of prosocial behavior and reductive contingencies for inappropriate behavior have not always increased positive interaction in families of conduct disordered children. In Taplin and Reid's (1977) study of aggressive boys, parents applied a "social reprogramming" intervention—behavior contracts, awarding of points and rewards for prosocial behaviors, and timeout for behavior problems. (However, it is unclear to what extent positive social interaction as we have defined it here was targeted.) Although maladaptive parent-child interactions (positive consequences for deviant and aversive consequences for prosocial behavior) were reduced, there was no change in parents' positive consequences for children's prosocial behavior.

Kelly, Embry, and Baer (1979) found a similar lack of effect of differential attention and further demonstrated that the problem child's positive social behavior to parents did not increase until parents were taught to support each other's use of behavior management techniques, and specific positive interactions between parents and child were arranged on a regular basis.

Finally, Wahler and Fox (1979) investigated the relative effects of social and independent toy play behavior contracts on behavior problems and positive interactions between several conduct disordered boys and their mothers. Social contracts involved reinforcing subjects for brief periods of appropriate play and interaction with their mothers. Independent play contracts called for reinforcing subjects for equivalent periods of appropriate solitary play. Although parent-child interaction increased under the social contract, there were concurrent increases in the boys' oppositional actions. The subsequent solitary play contract condition returned interaction to baseline levels and decreased oppositional behavior below baseline levels.

Withdrawn, autistic, and mentally retarded children. Published, empirical reports of home-based interventions designed to increase positive interaction between socially withdrawn children and their parents or siblings are virtually nonexistent. Studies with autistic children are a little more frequent.

Miller and Cantwell (1976) reported two case studies of sibling-mediated intervention, one of which involved a boy who was "moderately retarded with autistic features." Four older siblings were taught to use mild reprimands and timeout to eliminate the subject's food stealing. Also, each sibling was asked to spend 15 minutes each day in a one-to-one activity (playing cars, going for a walk) with the subject, during which time they were to "encourage eye contact, coherent speech, and appropriate social behaviors." Although quantitative measures of interaction and specifics of the encouragement procedures were not reported, arguing was reportedly decreased and positive interaction increased.

Hemsley et al. (1978) described long-term outcomes of a behavioral, home-based training program for families of autistic children. Although the specific interventions for teaching social interaction skills were not described, increases were noted in certain classes of mother-child interactive behavior—social language of the child and language-facilitating behaviors of the mother such as praise, corrections, prompting, questions, and expansions. However, other categories of interaction (play with mother, overall positive interaction) did not increase.

Finally, in a recent study by Blackman (1986), mothers of two handicapped girls were taught a set of procedures and target social initiations with which to increase positive interaction between their handicapped and nonhandicapped children. One handicapped subject had been identified as moderately retarded, socially withdrawn, and oppositional; the other had been diagnosed as autistic and was described by her parents as severely withdrawn and echolalic. The procedures (modeling, prompting, contingent praise) and target behaviors (verbally organizing play, sharing, assisting) were those initially developed for classrooms (Day, Lindeman, Powell, Fox, Stowitschek, & Shores, 1984; Day, Powell, & Stowitschek, 1980) and later modified for use with families (Powell, Salzberg, Rule, Levy, & Itzkowitz, 1983). Parents applied the procedures to both the handicapped and nonhandicapped siblings during a 10-minute training session. Two 5-minute generalization sessions were also conducted, one just before (delayed) and one just after (immediate) the training session to assess generalization of increased sibling interaction to occasions when intervention was not being applied. Previously, Powell et al. (1983) reported spontaneous transfer of increased sibling interaction to delayed, but not to immediate, generalization sessions. Although Blackman (1986) found increased interactions during training for both sibling dyads, there was little evidence of transfer to either generalization session.

In contrast to withdrawn and autistic children, mentally retarded children and their families have increasingly been the focus of applied social interaction research. Seitz and Terdal (1972) reported successful treatment of interactional problems between a mother and her young mentally retarded son in a clinic setting. During pretest observations, mother-child interactions were characterized by high rates of maternal instructions and child noncompliance. Child compliance and positive interaction increased following therapist modeling of how to praise, follow the child's lead, and decrease instructions. Similar increases in positive interaction were reported by Mash and Terdal (1973) who used group training procedures to teach more effective play skills and behavior modification techniques to several groups of mothers of handicapped children.

Christophersen and Sykes (1979) described a home-based program for three families of developmentally delayed children. Positive and negative interactions were observed at home before and after parents implemented a reward system for appropriate behavior and timeout for inappropriate behavior. Positive and negative interactions were very broadly defined and the specific behaviors for which these contingencies were arranged were not described. Subsequent to intervention,

---

In contrast to children who are withdrawn and autistic, children with mental retardation and their families have increasingly been the focus of applied social interaction research.

> Parent training taught parents to apply direct teaching tactics to teach the target behaviors and to increase sibling interaction.

positive interactions between all three subjects and their parents increased; negative interactions decreased for two of the three.

McCollum (1984) used modeling, videotaped feedback, and discussion to increase specific socially-directed maternal behaviors (facial movement toward the child, turn taking, vocal imitation of the child). These behaviors were thought likely to increase handicapped infants' and toddlers' vocalizations and toy play. Increases in the mothers' target behaviors were associated with increases in children's target behaviors. However, these increases did not transfer to generalization play situations between the mothers and children.

Peer interaction research has spawned several studies of sibling interactions of mentally retarded children. Powell et al. (1983) experimentally investigated a parent-mediated intervention (see above description) to increase positive interaction between their handicapped and nonhandicapped children. All handicapped subjects had been previously diagnosed as moderately mentally retarded and had been referred to the investigators due to deficits in sibling interaction. Target behaviors were sharing, verbally organizing play, assisting, rough and tumble, and affection—behaviors that facilitated positive responses from peers in classroom research (Tremblay et al., 1981). Reciprocal interactions were observed during a 10-minute session involving the subject, sibling, and parent (this later became the training time) and during a subsequent 15-minute generalization session including only the two children. Three conditions were implemented successively in a multiple baseline across families: Baseline, Initial Attempts, and Parent Training. In Initial Attempts, the experimenters simply asked parents, without any training, to do their best to get the children to play together. Parent Training taught parents to apply direct teaching tactics to teach the target behaviors and to increase sibling interaction. During Baseline and Initial Attempts there was little or no sibling interaction. Parent Training increased the frequency and duration of sibling play interactions markedly. Three of the four sibling dyads spontaneously increased their interactions during the generalization sessions.

Since the Powell et al. (1983) study, there have been several replications and extensions. In the first of a series of studies, Savelle, Fox, Spiegel-McGill, and Blackman (1986) attempted to identify the locus and durability of change in sibling interaction that might result from the interaction training procedures. Because Powell et al. (1983) used a single, broadly defined category of reciprocal interaction, it could not be determined if changes in interaction resulted from increases in handicapped children's, siblings', or both children's initiations. Also, Powell et al. did not assess the durability of these gains.

In our first case study (A-B design with follow-up), subjects were a 7-year-old moderately retarded girl, her 5-year-old normally developing sister, and their parents. Target behaviors, parent training, and intervention were the same as in the Powell et al. (1983) study. However, a continuous, sequential recording system noted the topography of social behavior (positive/negative, initiations/response, extended interaction) and the identity of the person (subject, sibling, parent) emitting the behavior. Second, parent intervention was gradually faded out, and follow-up observation was conducted 3 months after all intervention had ended. Both the subject and her sister increased their initiations and responses to one another as well as their extended interactions, the subject's initiations increasing more than those of her nonhandicapped sibling. Although both children's initiations decreased as the parent intervention was faded out, their extended interactions increased. At follow-up, initiations were within intervention frequencies; and although extended interactions had decreased, they remained above baseline levels.

In a later case study (Savelle et al., 1986), the effects of the social interaction training procedures on a moderately retarded boy with a history of predominately negative interactions with family members were evaluated. Observation and intervention procedures remained the same. When the mother began intervention, the handicapped boy's positive initiations to and interactions with his older sister increased. No consistent change was noted in the sibling's initiations. Withdrawal of intervention failed to completely reverse these interactions, clouding the demonstration of experimental control. Such failure to completely reverse increased social interactions is not unknown in social interaction research (see Hecimovic, Fox, Shores, & Strain, 1985) and may indicate the operation of any one of several processes, for instance, "entrapment" of the siblings in mutually reinforcing interactions (see Baer & Wolf, 1970; Kohler & Greenwood, 1986; McConnell, this issue) or reactivity to the observer.

More recently, James and Egel (1986) analyzed effects of a package of social interaction training procedures, using nonhandicapped siblings as the primary intervention agents. Participants were three socially withdrawn, handicapped children, their older nonhandicapped siblings, and a nonhandicapped friend of the sibling. The handicapped children were each 4 years old and were mentally retarded and/or physically handicapped. Siblings were 6 to 8 years of age. During intervention, the experimenters trained the nonhandicapped siblings to initiate interactions, prompt responses, and reinforce both initiations and responses by the handicapped child. Mothers learned to use response priming (a verbal reminder to play together) during generalization probes. Interval recording of initiations and reciprocal interactions were conducted in the home during (a) freeplay probes with the sibling dyads and experimenter; (b) generalization probes involving the sibling dyads, nonhandicapped friend, and parent (but excluding the experimenter); and (c) 6-month follow-up probes similar to the generalization probes. A multiple baseline across siblings analyzed the effects of the sibling-mediated intervention. Results showed that (a) the sibling-mediated intervention increased initiations and interactions between the siblings during freeplay probes and these gains persisted at the 6-month follow-up; (b) similar increases in sibling initiations and interactions occurred during generalization probes without intervention and response priming by the mother further magnified these generalization effects; (c) nonhandicapped friends' initiations to subjects increased slightly during generalization probes but handicapped subjects' initiations to the friend did not; and (d) across setting generalization of sibling interaction was also noted.

Summary and conclusions. To summarize, there have been comparatively few analyses of interventions designed to increase behaviorally disordered children's positive interactions with family members. This paucity of research is particularly evident for withdrawn and autistic children. Studies with conduct disordered children have produced mixed results, some showing that positive interactions with parents and siblings can be increased through

> There have been comparatively few analyses of interventions designed to increase the positive interactions between children with behavioral disorders and other family members.

> Child development theorists have often linked internalizing disorders such as social withdrawal to parent-child interaction patterns.

some form of differential reinforcement of appropriate interaction either alone or in combination with reductive contingencies for negative behaviors (Lavigueur, 1976; Leitenberg et al., 1977; O'Leary et al., 1967) while others have not (Kelly et al., 1979; Taplin & Reid, 1977). At least one study has shown that increasing positive interaction between *some* conduct disordered children and their families had unintended negative side effects on problem behavior (Wahler & Fox, 1979).

The authors of this article were unable to find any family-based intervention studies of socially withdrawn children. Socially withdrawn children have been frequent targets of intervention studies in classroom settings (Odom & DeKlyan, in press; Strain & Fox, 1981). Also, child development theorists have often linked internalizing disorders such as social withdrawal to parent-child interaction patterns (e.g., Becker, 1964). Although the data supporting this link are tenuous (Becker, 1964; Hetherington & Martin, 1979), recent research suggests that a child's scores on laboratory measures of maternal attachment predict sociability with peers. Consequently, the lack of family-based intervention studies with withdrawn children is surprising. There remains a need to identify and experimentally analyze parent and sibling behaviors which may facilitate the social behavior development of withdrawn children.

Equally surprising is the rarity of studies with autistic children, especially given the central role of impaired social responsiveness in autism. Social withdrawal is one of the primary defining characteristics of the disorder (Kanner, 1943; Kauffman, 1985), a major concern of parents (DeMyer, 1979), and a critical factor in the integration of severely handicapped persons into more normalized environments (Brady, Gunter, McEvoy, Shores, & Fox, 1984). The outcomes of the few family-based intervention studies of autistic children are promising. Given training, parents (Blackman, 1986; Hemsley et al., 1978) or siblings (Miller & Cantwell, 1976) can intervene to increase positive interactions with an autistic family member. However, several cautions are in order. With the exception of the Blackman study, intervention procedures leading to improved social interaction have not been well specified.

A somewhat similar problem exists in terms of the locus of social behavior change. As Gaylord-Ross and Haring note elsewhere in this issue, it is important that interventions not only increase interaction between autistic and nonhandicapped persons, but that they also teach the handicapped person to initiate and reasonably sustain interactions.

Finally, the small number of children and families studied puts at issue the replicability and generality of these results for the larger population of families with autistic children. Again, there is an obvious need for further family-based intervention research with autistic children.

This is not to say that the need for family-based approaches to social development is going unheeded. In fact, over the past decade a number of publications have discussed the nature and implications of autistic withdrawal for the family and have described clinical programs that address the social needs of autistic children and their families (see for example, Rutter & Schopler, 1978; Schopler & Mesibov, 1984, 1986). However, it seems that what we do lack is an adequate empirical base for family intervention that identifies target social skills, environmental contexts, and efficient intervention procedures for enhancing the social development of autistic children and adolescents.

The slightly larger body of intervention research with mentally retarded children and their families is of some help in this respect. Generally, these intervention procedures have been more specifically described and the studies more controlled. Again, the results are encouraging. Both parents (Christophersen & Sykes, 1979; Mash & Terdal, 1973; McCollum, 1984; Powell et al., 1983; Savelle et al., 1986; Seitz & Terdal, 1972) and siblings (James & Egel, 1986) have successfully applied learning theory-based interventions to increase positive interactions with mentally retarded children. Indeed, family researchers have already begun to apply and evaluate generalization and maintenance programming techniques, such as response priming (James & Egel, 1986) and fading of intervention tactics (Savelle et al., 1986). There may, however, be limits to the applicability of these studies to families with autistic children. Potential limiting factors include the degree and specific nature of social withdrawal (Strain & Fox, 1981) and the presence of competing or aberrant responses (Donnellan et al., 1984; Lichstein & Wahler, 1976).

In the studies reviewed, few of the mentally retarded subjects appeared unresponsive to parents' or siblings' social overtures when they occurred nor were many characterized as engaging in high rates of stereotypic or other aberrant behavior. It remains to be seen if and how existing social intervention procedures will need to be modified for children who exhibit more extreme withdrawal (less responsiveness to or active avoidance of social overtures) and/or who engage in high rates of stereotypic and other aberrant behavior.

Finally, there are research issues and needs that cut across categorical boundaries. We briefly pose these as a series of questions below.

1. What are the behavioral targets that if taught will facilitate and perhaps "entrap" behaviorally disordered children and their siblings or parents into positive interaction? Will the social initiation targets which effect peer interaction (Strain, 1983; Tremblay et al., 1981) serve a similar function in sibling or parent interaction? So far the outcomes have been quite positive in those family-based studies where these social initiation skills have been targeted (Blackman, 1986; Powell et al., 1983; Savelle et al., 1986). On the other hand, recent descriptive analyses of normally developing children suggest that sibling and peer interactions differ in terms of social roles assumed by the interactants—teacher, manager, playmate, initiator, responder (Abramovitch et al., 1986; Brody, Stoneman, MacKinnon, & MacKinnon, 1985; Stoneman, Brody, & MacKinnon, 1984). What is currently needed are studies of children that descriptively and experimentally analyze the social effects of particular behaviors much as Strain (1983) and Tremblay et al., (1981) conducted in preschool settings.

2. What of the contexts in which researchers have sought to increase family interaction? With few exceptions, researchers have analyzed and intervened upon behaviorally disordered children's interactions in play situations. Can or should we reasonably expect children to engage in longer and longer bouts of play interaction, especially when observational data indicate that normally developing sibling pairs spend a considerable amount of time in solitary play (e.g., Mash & Mercer, 1979;

Parents and siblings have successfully applied learning theory-based interventions to increase positive interactions with children with mental retardation.

> The current gaps in our empirical knowledge about family interaction are wide and complicated by the fact that direct, observation-based studies of families are by no means easy to implement.

Savelle et al., 1986)? What are the various activities and situations in which sibling and parent interactions typically take place? A variety of contexts other than play can serve as occasions for interactions including television watching (Brody & Stoneman, 1983; Brody, Stoneman, & Sanders, 1980; Stoneman & Brody, 1983), going for walks (Miller & Cantwell, 1976), and dinnertime conversation. How, if at all, can these situations be used as opportunities for improving family interactions of behaviorally disordered children and how may improvements in interaction in one of these home situations affect interaction in another?

3. If interaction between behaviorally disordered children and their siblings or parents increases, what if any effects accrue to their interactions with other relatives, neighborhood children, or their classmates and teachers at school? James and Egel (1986) noted modest generalization of increases in retarded subjects' sibling interaction to interactions with a neighborhood friend during specially arranged play sessions and this is encouraging. However, other descriptive (Abramovitch et al., 1986; Bernal et al., 1976; Lichstein & Wahler, 1976) and intervention (Wahler, 1975) studies have found little across setting or person generalization of interaction patterns.

4. It is now almost trite to say that there is a need for generalization and maintenance research. However, it is true that social interaction interventions have been quite effective at producing situational change and less reliable in creating broader, more durable impact on social development. Techniques for "programming" generalization and maintenance of social behavior gains are available and have tentative empirical support. These include multiple exemplar training (e.g., Brady, Shores et al., 1984; Fox et al., 1984; Gaylord-Ross, Haring, Breen, & Pitts-Conway, 1984) and response-dependent fading of intervention tactics (e.g., Fox, Shores, Lindeman, & Strain, 1986; Timm, Strain, & Eller, 1979). Certain of these techniques (i.e., intervention fading tactics) and others such as response priming have also begun to be applied in families of handicapped withdrawn children (James & Egel, 1986; Savelle et al., 1986). What is needed then are additional systematic analyses of the generalization and maintenance effects of these and other similar tactics and of the settings and persons of whom generalization can be achieved. In many respects, the James and Egel (1986) study provides future researchers with an exemplary model.

These and many other questions confront those who would attempt a more comprehensive understanding of the social development of behaviorally disordered children. As we have tried to point out, the current gaps in our empirical knowledge about family interaction are wide. This is complicated by the fact that direct, observation-based studies of families are by no means easy to implement. Yet, the studies reviewed illustrate that such research can be done and give a foundation upon which to increase the database. Hopefully, the issues and questions raised will serve as a point of departure and debate if not something of a guide for future research.

REFERENCES

Abramovitch, R., Corter, C., Peppler, D., & Stanhope, L. (1986). Sibling and peer interaction: A final follow-up and a comparison. *Child Development, 57,* 217-229.

Arnold, J., Levine, A., Patterson, G. (1975). Changes in sibling behavior following family intervention. *Journal of Consulting and Clinical Psychology, 43,* 683-688.

Baer, D., & Wolf, M. (1970). The entry into natural communities of reinforcement. In R. Ulrich, T. Stachnik, & J. Mabry (Eds.), *Control of human behavior, from cure to prevention* (Vol. 2, pp. 319-324). Glenview, IL: Scott-Foresman.

Becker, W. (1964). Consequences of different kinds of parental discipline. In M. Hoffman & L. Hoffman (Eds.), *Review of child development research* (Vol. 1, pp. 169-208). New York: Russell Sage Foundation.

Bernal, M., Delfini, L., North, J., & Kreutzer, S. (1976). Comparison of boys' behaviors in homes and classrooms. In E. Mash, L. Hamerlynck, & L. Handy (Eds.), *Behavior modification and families* (pp. 204-227). New York: Brunner-Mazel.

Bijou, S., Peterson, R., & Ault, M. (1968). A method to integrate descriptive and experimental field studies at the level of data and empirical concepts. *Journal of Applied Behavior Analysis, 1,* 175-191.

Blackman, J. (1986). *Parent-mediated treatment of exceptional children's social withdrawal.* Unpublished doctoral dissertation, George Peabody College for Teachers of Vanderbilt University.

Bower, E., & Lambert, N. (1961). *A process for inschool screening of children with emotional handicaps.* Princeton, NJ: Educational Testing Service.

Brady, M. P., Gunter, P., McEvoy, M. A., Shores, R. E., & Fox, J. J. (1984). Considerations for socially integrated school environments for severely handicapped students. *Education and Training of the Mentally Retarded, 19,* 246-253.

Brady, M. P., Shores, R. E., Gunter, P., McEvoy, M. A., Fox, J. J., White, C. (1984). Generalization of an adolescent's social interaction behavior via multiple peers in a classroom setting. *Journal of the Association for Severe Handicaps, 9,* 278-286.

Brody, G., & Stoneman, Z. (1983). The influence of television viewing on family interactions. *Journal of Family Issues, 4,* 329-348.

Brody, G., Stoneman, Z., & MacKinnon, C. (1982). Role asymmetries in interactions among school-aged children, their younger siblings, and their friends. *Child Development, 53,* 1364-1370.

Brody, G., Stoneman, Z., MacKinnon, C., & MacKinnon, R. (1985). Role relationships and behavior between preschool-aged and school-aged sibling pairs. *Developmental Psychology, 21,* 124-129.

Brody, G., Stoneman, Z., & Sanders, A. (1980). Effects of television viewing on family interactions: An observational study. *Family Relations, 29,* 216-220.

Campbell, H. (1986). Morbid shyness. *The British Medical Journal, 2,* 805-807.

Christophersen, E., & Stykes, B. (1979). An intensive, home-based family training program for developmentally-delayed children. In L. Hamerlynck (Ed.), *Behavioral systems for the developmentally delayed. Vol. 1. School and family environments* (pp. 89-101). New York: Brunner-Mazel.

Corter, C., Abramovitch, R., & Pepler, D. (1983). The role of the mother in sibling interaction. *Child Development, 54,* 1599-1605.

Day, R., Fox, J. J., Shores, R. E., Lindeman, D., & Stowitschek, J. (1983). The social competence intervention project: Developing educational procedures for teaching social interaction skills to handicapped children. *Behavioral Disorders, 8,* 120-127.

Day, R., Lindeman, D., Powell, T., Fox, J. J., Stowitschek, J., & Shores, R. E. (1984). Empirically-derived teaching package for socially withdrawn handicapped and nonhandicapped children. *Teacher Education and Special Education, 7,* 46-55.

Day, R., Powell, T., & Stowitschek, J. (1980). *The social competence intervention package for preschool youngsters.* Nashville, TN: George Peabody College for Teachers at Vanderbilt University.

Delfini, L., Bernal, M., & Rosen, P. (1976). Comparison of deviant and normal boys in home settings. In E. Mash, L. Hamerlynck, & L. Handy (Eds.), *Behavior modification and families* (pp. 228-248). New York: Brunner-Mazel.

DeMyer, M. (1979). *Parents and children in autism.* New York: John Wiley & Sons.

Donnellan, A., Anderson, J., & Mesaros, R. (1984). An observational study of stereotypic behavior and proximity related to the occurrence of autistic child-family member interactions. *Journal of Autism and Developmental Disorders, 14,* 205-210.

Dunn, J., & Kendrick, C. (1982*). Siblings: Love, envy, and understanding.* Cambridge, MA: Harvard University Press.

Eheart, B. (1982). Mother-child interactions with nonretarded and mentally retarded preschoolers. *American Journal of Mental Deficiency, 87,* 20-25.

Finch, M., & Hops, H. (1983). Remediation of social withdrawal in young children: Considerations for the practitioner. *Child and Youth Services, 5,* 29-42.

Foster, S., & Ritchey, W. (1979). Issues in the assessment of social competence in children. *Journal of Applied Behavior Analysis, 12,* 625-638.

Fox, J. J., Day, R., & McEvoy, M. A. (in press). An empirically-based educational approach to developing social competence in young children: Outcomes and issues. *Childhood Education.*

Fox, J. J., Gunter, P., Brady, M. P., Bambara, L., Spiegel-McGill, P., & Shores, R. E. (1984). Using multiple peer exemplars to develop generalized social responding of an autistic girl. In. R. B. Rutherford & C. M. Nelson (Eds.), *Severe behavior disorders of children and youth* (Vol. 7, pp. 17-27). Reston, VA: Council for Children with Behavioral Disorders.

Fox, J. J., Shores, R. E., Lindeman, D., & Strain, P. (1986). The effects of response dependent fading procedures in developing and maintaining social initiations of withdrawn preschool children. *Journal of Abnormal Child Psychology, 14,* 387-396.

Gaylord-Ross, R., Haring, T., Breen, C., & Pitts-Conway, V. (1984). The training and generalizations of social interaction skills with autistic youth. *Journal of Applied Behavior Analysis, 17,* 229-247.

Gordon, S., & Davidson, N. (1981). Behavioral parent training. In A. Gurman & D. Kniskern (Eds.), *Handbook of family therapy* (pp. 515-575). New York: Brunner-Mazel.

Hartup, W. (1970). Peer interaction and social organization. In P. Mussen (Ed.), *Carmichael's manual of child psychology* (Vol. 2, pp. 361-456). New York: John Wiley & Sons.

Hartup, W. (1983). Peer relations. In P. Mussen (Series Ed.), *Handbook of child psychology* (4th ed., pp. 167-172). New York: John Wiley & Sons.

Hawkins, R., Peterson, R., Schweid, E., & Bijou, S. (1966). Behavior therapy in the home: Amelioration of problem parent-child relations with the parent in a therapeutic role. *Journal of Experimental Child Psychology, 4,* 99-107.

Hecimovic, A., Fox, J. J., Shores, R. E., & Strain, P. (1985). An analysis of developmentally integrated and segregated freeplay settings and the generalization of newly-acquired social behaviors of socially withdrawn preschoolers. *Behavioral Assessment, 7,* 1367-388.

Hemsley, R., Howlin, P., Berger, M., Hersov, L., Holbrook, D., Rutter, M., & Yule, W. (1978). Treating autistic children in a family context. In M. Rutter & E. Schopler (Eds.), *Autism: A reappraisal of concepts and treatment* (pp. 379-411). New York: Plenum.

Hetherington, M., & Martin, B. (1979). Family interaction. In H. Quay & J. Werry (Eds.), *Psychopathological disorders of childhood* (2nd ed., pp. 247-302). New York: John Wiley & Sons.

Hops, H. (1982). Social skills training for socially withdrawn/isolate children. In P. Karoly & J. Steffen (Eds*.), Improving children's competence: Advances in child behavior analysis* (Vol. 1, pp. 39-101). Lexington, MA: Heath.

James, S., & Egel, A. (1986). A direct prompting strategy for increasing reciprocal interactions between handicapped and nonhandicapped siblings. *Journal of Applied Behavior Analysis, 19,* 173-186.

Kanner, L. (1943). Autistic disturbances of affective contact. *Nervous Child, 2,* 217-250.

Kanner, L. (1971). Follow-up study of eleven children originally reported in 1943. *Journal of Autism and Childhood Schizophrenia, 1,* 119-145.

Kanner, L., Rodriguez, A., & Ashenden, B. (1972). How far can autistic children go in matters of social adaptation? *Journal of Autism and Childhood Schizophrenia, 2,* 9-33.

Kauffman, J. (1985). *Characteristics of children's behavior disorders* (3rd ed., pp. 1-25, 66-81). Columbus, OH: Merrill.

Kelly, M., Embry, L., & Baer, D. (1979). Skills for child management and family support. *Behavior Modification, 3,* 373-396.

Kohler, F., & Greenwood, C. (1986). Toward a technology of generalization: The identification of natural contingencies of reinforcement. *Behavior Analyst, 9,* 19-26.

Lamb, M. (1978). The development of sibling relationships in infancy: A short-term longitudinal study. *Child Development, 49,* 1189-1196.

Lavigueur, H. (1976). The use of siblings as an adjunct to the behavioral treatment of children in the home with parents as therapists. *Behavior Therapy, 7,* 607-613.

Leitenberg, H., Burchard, J., Burchard, S., Fuller, E., & Lysaght, T. (1977). Using positive reinforcement to suppress behavior: Some experimental comparisons with sibling conflict. *Behavior Therapy, 8,* 168-172.

Lichstein, K., & Wahler, R. (1976). The ecological assessment of an autistic child. *Journal of Abnormal Child Psychology, 4,* 31-54.

Maccoby, E., & Martin, J. (1983). Socialization in the context of the family: Parent-child interaction. In P. Mussen (Series Ed.), *Handbook of child psychology* (4th ed., pp. 1-101). New York: John Wiley & Sons.

Martin, S., & Graunke, B. (1979). A behavioral analysis of the home environment of autistic children. In L. Hamerlynck (Ed.), *Behavioral systems for the developmentally delayed: Vol. 1. School and family environments* (pp. 172-192). New York: Brunner-Mazel.

Mash, E., & Mercer, B. (1979). A comparison of deviant and nondeviant boys while playing alone and interacting with a sibling. *Journal of Child Psychology and Psychiatry and Allied Disciplines, 20,* 197-207.

Mash, E., & Terdal, L. (1973). Modification of mother-child interactions: Playing with children. *Mental Retardation, 11,* 44-49.

McCollum, J. (1984). Social interaction between parents and babies: Validation of an intervention procedure. *Child: Care, health, and development, 10,* 301-315.

Michaelson, L., & Mannarino, A. (1986). Social skills training with children: Research and clinical application. In P. Strain, M. Guralnick, & H. Walker (Eds.), *Children's social behavior. Development, assessment, and modification* (pp. 373-406). Orlando, FL: Academic Press.

Miller, N., & Cantwell, D. (1976). Sibling as therapist: A behavioral approach. *American Journal of Psychiatry, 133,* 447-450.

Odom, S., & DeKlyen, M. (in press). Social withdrawal in childhood. In G. Adams (Ed.), *Behavior disorders: Theory and characteristics.* Englewood Cliffs, NJ: Prentice-Hall.

O'Leary, K., O'Leary, S., & Becker, W. (1967). Modification of a deviant sibling interaction pattern in the home. *Behavior Research and Therapy, 5,* 113-120.

Patterson, G. (1976). The aggressive child: Victim and architect of a coercive system. In L. Hamerlynck, L. Handy, & E. Mash (Eds.), *Behavior modification and families: Theory and research* (Vol. 1, pp. 267-316). New York: Brunner-Mazel.

Patterson, G. (1980). Mothers: The unacknowledged victims. *Monographs of the Society for Research in Child Development, 44*(5, Serial No. 186).

Patterson, G. (1982). *Coercive family processes.* Eugene, OR: Castalia.

Patterson, G., Ray, R., Shaw, D, & Cobb, J. (1969). *Family observation code.* Unpublished manuscript, University of Oregon, Eugene.

Powell, T., Salzberg, C., Rule, S., Levy, S., & Itzkowitz, J. (1983). Teaching mentally retarded children to play with their siblings using parents as trainers. *Education and Treatment of Children, 6,* 343-362.

Quay, H. (1979). Classification. In H. Quay & J. Werry (Eds.), *Psychopathological disorders of childhood* (2nd ed., pp. 1-42). New York: John Wiley & Sons.

Rutter, M., & Schopler, E. (1978). *Autism: A reappraisal of concepts and treatment.* New York: Plenum..

Savelle, S., Fox, J. J., & Phillips, M. (1987, March). *Handicapped and nonhandicapped children's social interactions with their siblings: A preliminary descriptive analysis.* Paper presented at the Gatlinburg Conference on Research and Theory in Mental Retardation and Developmental Disabilities, Gatlinburg, TN.

Schopler, E., & Mesibov, G. (1984). *The effects of autism on the family.* New York: Plenum.

Schopler, E., & Mesibov, G. (1986). Introduction to social behavior in autism. In E. Schopler & G. Mesibov (Eds.), *Social behavior in autism* (pp. 1-11). New York: Plenum.

Seitz, S., & Terdal, L. (1972). A modeling to changing parent-child interactions. *Mental Retardation, 10,* 39-43.

Snyder, J. (1977). Reinforcement analysis of interaction in problem and nonproblem families. *Journal of Abnormal Psychology, 86,* 528-535.

Stoneman, Z., & Brody, G. (1983). Family interactions during three programs. *Journal of Family Issues, 4,* 349-365.

Stoneman, Z., & Brody, G. (in press). Observational research on mentally retarded children, three parents, and their siblings. In S. Lanesman & P. Vietze (Eds.), *Living environments and mental retardation.* Washington, DC: AAMD.

Stoneman, Z., Brody, G., & Abbott, D. (1983). In-home observations of young Down's syndrome children with their mothers and fathers. *American Journal of Mental Deficiency, 87,* 591-600.

Stoneman, Z., Brody, G., Davis, C., & Crapps, J. (1986, April). *Mentally retarded children and their older siblings: Role relationships and responsibilities.* Paper presented at the Conference on Human Development, Vanderbilt University, Nashville, TN.

Stoneman, Z., Brody, G., & MacKinnon, C. (1984). Naturalistic observations of children's activities and roles while playing with their siblings and friends. *Child Development, 55,* 617-627.

Strain, P. (1983). Identification of social skill curriculum targets for severely handicapped children in mainstream preschools. *Applied Research in Mental Retardation, 4,* 369-382.

Strain, P., & Fox, J. (1981). Peers as behavior change agents for withdrawn classmates. In B. Lahey & A. Kazdin (Eds.), *Advances in clinical child psychology* (Vol. 4, pp. 167-198). New York: Plenum.

Strain, P., Guralnick, M., & Walker, H. (1986). *Children's social behavior and development: Assessment and modification.* Orlando: Academic Press.

Taplin, P., & Reid, J. (1977). Changes in parent consequation as a function of family interaction. *Journal of Consulting and Clinical Psychology, 4,* 973-981.

Terdal, L., Jackson, R., & Garner, A. (1976). Mother-child interactions: A comparison between normal and developmentally delayed groups. In E. Mash, L. Hamerlynck, & L. Handy (Eds.), *Behavior modification and families* (pp. 249-264). New York: Brunner-Mazel.

Timm, M., Strain, P., & Eller, P. (1979). Effects of systematic response-dependent fading and thinning on the maintenance of child-child interaction. *Journal of Applied Behavior Analysis, 12,* 308.

Tramblay, A., Strain, P., Hendrickson, J., & Shores, R. E. (1981). Social interactions of normally developing preschool children: Using normative data for subject and target behavior selection. *Behavior Modification, 5,* 237-253.

Van Hasselt, V., Hersen, M., Whitehill, M., & Bellack, A. (1979). Social skill assessment and training for children: An evaluative review. *Behavior Research and Therapy, 17,* 413-437.

Wahler, R. (1975). Some structural aspects of deviant child behavior. *Journal of Applied Behavior Analysis, 8,* 27-42.

Wahler, R., & Fox, J. J. (1979). Solitary toy play and timeout: A family treatment package for children with aggressive and oppositional behavior. *Journal of Applied Behavior Analysis, 13,* 23-39.

Wahler, R., House, A., & Stambaugh, E. (1976). *Ecological assessment of child problem behavior: A clinical package for home, school, and institutional settings.* New York: Pergamon.

Structured Learning: A Psychoeducational Approach for Teaching Social Competencies

Arnold P. Goldstein
Robert P. Sprafkin
Jane Gershaw
Paul Klein

ABSTRACT: This article describes the use of Structured Learning, a psychoeducational approach for teaching social competencies to adolescents and preadolescents. The youngsters who are likely to be trained through Structured Learning are generally categorized as aggressive, withdrawn, immature, or developmentally lagging. Research evidence evaluating the effectiveness of this approach is also discussed.

Reprinted from *Behavioral Disorders, Vol. 8, Number 3,* May 1983, pp. 161-170

Psychological education, or what many are coming to refer to as the *psychoeducational movement,* has been gaining an undeniable foothold within teacher training for many years. Growing out of the personal development context which nurtured such earlier movements as progressive education (Dewey, 1938) and character education (Chapman, 1977), a number of psychoeducational approaches have emerged. These approaches generally deal with teaching concepts and behaviors relevant to values, morality, and emotional development. Such programs as moral education (Kohlberg, 1973), values clarification (Simon, Howe, & Kirschenbaum, 1972), effective education (Miller, 1976), and identity education (Weinstein & Fantini, 1970) are contemporary examples of this educational direction. They share concerns with the facilitation of social effectiveness, personal development, and competence within educational curricula. As Authier, Gustafson, Guerney, and Kastorf (1975) observed, many individuals would prefer to restrict formal education to the traditional 3R's and leave such concerns as morality, coping skills, and other aspects of social competence to others (e.g., parents, religious organizations). However, the demand for teachers and schools to meet these needs in youngsters is evident and increasing.

One psychoeducational approach known as Structured Learning has gained considerable attention in recent years (Cartledge & Milburn, 1980; Goldstein, Sprafkin, Gershaw & Klein, 1980; Larsen, in press; Rathjen & Foreyt, 1980). Structured Learning consists of four major components,

> Skill deficiencies are most likely to be manifested in problems of aggressiveness, withdrawal, immaturity, and associated difficulties in surmounting developmental hurdles.

each of which has a strong empirical basis in psychology. These components are: (a) modeling, (b) role playing, (c) performance feedback, and (d) transfer of training. In Structured Learning, youngsters' interpersonal, affective, coping, and planning behaviors are viewed as *skills* in which they may be proficient or nonproficient. The task of Structured Learning is to teach these skills when youngsters are deficient in them. Skills taught via Structured Learning are divided into six groups.

Group I— Beginning Social Skills
1. Listening
2. Starting a conversation
3. Having a conversation
4. Asking a question
5. Saying thank you
6. Introducing yourself
7. Introducing other people
8. Giving a compliment

Group II— Advanced Social Skills
9. Asking for help
10. Joining in
11. Giving instructions
12. Following instructions
13. Apologizing
14. Convincing others

Group III—Skills for Dealing with Feelings
15. Knowing your feelings
16. Expressing your feelings
17. Understanding the feelings of others
18. Dealing with someone else's anger
19. Expressing affection
20. Dealing with fear
21. Rewarding yourself

Group IV—Skill Alternatives to Aggression
22. Asking permission
23. Sharing something
24. Helping others
25. Negotiating
26. Using self-control
27. Standing up for your rights
28. Responding to teasing
29. Avoiding trouble with others
30. Keeping out of fights

Group V— Skills for Dealing with Stress
31. Making a complaint
32. Answering a complaint
33. Sportsmanship after the game
34. Dealing with embarrassment
35. Dealing with being left out
36. Standing up for a friend
37. Responding to persuasion
38. Responding to failure
39. Dealing with confusing messages
40. Dealing with an accusation
41. Getting ready for a difficult conversation
42. Dealing with group pressure

Group VI—Planning Skills
43. Deciding on something to do
44. Deciding on what caused a problem
45. Setting a goal
46. Deciding on your abilities
47. Gathering information
48. Arranging problems by importance
49. Making a decision
50. Concentrating on a task

Skill deficiencies are most likely to be manifested in problems of aggressiveness, withdrawal, immaturity, and associated difficulties in surmounting developmental hurdles.

Structured Learning is a group technique, generally involving five to eight youngsters plus one or two trainers. Adaptations for using Structured Learning in regular-sized classes have also been made. The approach has been used most extensively in regular and special education classes in junior and senior high schools or upper-level grades in elementary schools. Structured

Learning trainers have usually been drawn from the ranks of regular and special education teachers. This latter group has shown particular interest in Structured Learning because of its compatibility with the requirements of Public Law 94-142. Skill acquisition is geared toward enabling handicapped youngsters to function better within the least restrictive, most normal environment. As Structured Learning is behaviorally oriented, its procedures are able to be assessed in observable, concrete terms necessary for the development of Individual Education Plans (IEPs), and for measuring progress in youngster's skill acquisition.

TRAINING PROCEDURES
Modeling

Teaching a skill begins by exposing groups of youngsters to vivid examples (live on video or audio tape, filmsor filmstrip) of the skill being used well. This constitutes the *modeling* component. Modeling displays present scenes or vignettes in which the protagonist handles potentially troublesome situations successfully by employing the skill being taught. One skill is taught at a time, so that the modeling vignettes depict several examples of a single skill being used in different situations. To make a skill presentation as concrete as possible, the skill is broken down into its component behavioral steps, each of which is illustrated in the modeling vignette. Youngsters' skill deficits are assessed via self-reports, observer's reports, and for research purposes, situational behavioral tests.

Role Playing

Following the presentation of the modeling display, a group discussion ensues. Youngsters are urged to comment on what they have seen and heard, and to relate the modeling of the skill to times in their own lives when use of the particular skill has been difficult. From the material generated in these discussions, *role plays* are developed. Each youngster is given an opportunity to role play or practice the skill as a rehearsal for a situation that might actually occur in a real-life circumstance. Thus role playing is presented as practice or rehearsal for future skill use. Each youngster in the main actor role gets an opportunity to choose as a co-actor someone who resembles the real-life protagonist or antagonist in as many ways as possible, and to enact the skill following the behavioral steps which constitute the skill. Considerable coaching and support is provided by the trainers throughout the role play.

Performance Feedback

Following the enactment of the role play, the trainers *elicit performance feedback* (approval, praise, constructive criticism) from the other group members. In general in this phase, the main actor is given support as well as helpful suggestions on how his or her performance might be made even more effective. At times the trainer may have the main actor replay the scene immediately so that the feedback from the other youngsters (and/or the trainers) may be incorporated without delay.

Transfer of Training

Finally, in a forthright effort to effect *transfer of training*, or transfer of the skill into the youngsters' real-life behavioral repertoire, a variety of procedures are implemented:

1. Provision of general principles. Transfer of training has been demonstrated to be facilitated by providing trainees with general mediating principles governing successful or competent performance on the training and criterion tasks. This procedure has typically been operationalized in laboratory contexts by

---

Social skills training procedures include modeling, role-playing, performance feedback, and transfer of training.

> The greater the similarity of physical and interpersonal stimuli in the Structured Learning setting and the school, home, or other setting in which the skill is to be applied, the greater the likelihood of transfer.

providing subjects with the organizing concepts, principles, strategies, or rationales that explain or account for the stimulus-response relationships operative in both the training and application settings. The provision of general principles to Structured Learning trainees is being operationalized in our training by the presentation in verbal, pictorial, and written forms of appropriate information governing skill instigation, selection, and implementation principles.

2. Overlearning. Overlearning is a procedure whereby learning is extended over more trials than are necessary merely to produce initial changes in the subjects' behavior. The overlearning, or repetition of successful skill enactment, in the typical Structured Learning session is quite substantial, with the given skill taught and its behavioral steps (a) modeled several times, (b) role played one or more times by the trainee, (c) observed live by the trainee as every other group member role plays it, (d) read by the trainee from a blackboard and on the Skill Card, (e) written by the trainee in his or her Trainee's Notebook, (f) practiced in vivo one or more times by the trainee as part of the formal homework assignment, (g) practiced in vivo one or more times by the trainee in response to adult and/or peer leader coaching, and (h) practiced in vivo one or more times by the trainee in response to skill-oriented, intrinsically interesting stimuli introduced into his or her real-life environment.

3. Identical elements. In perhaps the earliest experimental concern with transfer enhancement, Thorndike and Woodworth (1901) concluded that when there was a facilitative effect of one habit on another, it was to the extent that and because they shared identical elements. Ellis (1965) and Osgood (1953) have more recently emphasized the importance of transfer of similarity between stimulus and response aspects of the training and application tasks. The greater the similarity of physical and interpersonal stimuli in the Structured Learning setting and the school, home, or other setting in which the skill is to be applied, the greater the likelihood of transfer.

The "real-lifeness" of Structured Learning is operationalized in a number of ways. These operational expressions of identical elements include (a) the relevant and realistic content and portrayal of the models, protagonists, andsituations in the modeling displays tapes, all designed to be highly similar to what trainees are likely to face in their daily lives; (b) the physical props used in and the arrangement of the role-playing setting to be similar to the real-life settings; (c) the choice, coaching, and enactment of the co-actors or protagonists to be similar to real-life figures; (d) the manner in which the role plays themselves are conducted to be as responsive as possible to the real-life interpersonal stimuli to which the trainee will actually respond with the given skill, and to provide behavioral rehearsal of that skill as he/she actually plans to employ it; (e) the in vivo homework—coached and practiced in the training group, completed in the real-world setting, and reported upon in the training group in the immediately following session; and (f) the training of living units (all the members of a given class or cottage) as a unit.

4. Stimulus variability. Callantine and Warren (1955), Duncan (1959), and Shore and Sechrest (1961) have each demonstrated that positive transfer is greater when a variety of relevant training stimuli are employed. Stimulus variability is implemented in our Structured Learning studies by (a) rotation of group leaders across groups, (b) rotation of trainees across groups, (c) having trainees re-role play a given skill with several co-actors, (d) having trainees re-role play a given skill across several relevant settings, and (e) use of multiple homework assignments for each given skill.

5. Real-life reinforcement. Given successful implementation of both appropriate Structured Learning procedures and the transfer enhancement procedures examined above, positive transfer may still fail to occur. As Agras (1967), Gruber (1971), Patterson (1963), and Tharp and Wetzel (1969), and literally dozens of other investigators have shown, stable and enduring performance in application settings of newly learned skills is very much at the mercy of real-life reinforcement contingencies.

We have found it useful to implement several supplemental programs outside of the Structured Learning setting to help provide the rewards of reinforcements trainees need so that their new behaviors are maintained. These programs include provision for both external social reward (provided by people in the trainee's real-life environment) and self-reward (provided by the trainee himself or herself).

In several schools, juvenile detention centers, and other agencies, we have actively sought to identify and develop environmental or external support by holding orientation meetings for staff and for relatives and friends of trainees (i.e., the real-life reward and punishment givers). The purpose of these meetings was to acquaint significant others in the trainees' life with Structured Learning theory and procedures. Most important in these sessions is the presentation of procedures whereby staff, relatives, and friends can encourage and reward trainees as they practice their new skills. We consider these orientation sessions for such persons to be a major value for transfer of training.

Frequently, environmental support is insufficient to maintain newly learned skills. It is also the case that many real-life environments in which trainees work and live will actively resist the trainees' efforts at behavior change. For this reason, we have found it useful to include in our transfer efforts a program of self-reinforcement. Trainees can be instructed in the nature of self-reinforcement and encouraged to "say something and do something nice for yourself" if they practice their new skill well.

The five transfer-enhancement procedures we have briefly described above do not exhaust the actual range of techniques employed for such purposes that we have examined in our research program. A complete listing of these procedures, with citation of our research program's investigations) demonstrating their transfer-enhancing efficacy, are listed in Table 1 (Goldstein, 1981).

TABLE 1
Successful Transfer-Enhancing Procedures

1. Overlearning (Lopez, 1977)
2. Helper role structuring (Litwack, 1977; Solomon, 1978)
3. Identical elements (Wood, 1977; Guzzetta, 1974)
4. Coping modeling (Fleming, 1976)
5. Stimulus variability (Hummel, 1977)
6. General principles (Lopez, 1977; Lack, 1975)
7. Programmed reinforcement (Gutride, Goldstein, & Hunter, 1973; Greenleaf, 1977)
8. In vivo feedback (Goldstein & Goedhart, 1973)
9. Teaching skills in tandem (reciprocal benefits) (Hummel, 1977)
10. Mastery induction (Solomon, 1977)

> We have found it useful to implement several supplemental programs outside of the Structured Learning setting to help provide the rewards of reinforcements trainees need so that their new behaviors are maintained.

> In Structured Learning groups, group members may actively resist participation as prescribed, may participate but inappropriately, or may display one or another form of inactivity or hyperactivity.

All of these demonstrated transfer-enhancing techniques, as well as a substantial number of potentially fruitful techniques, are examined at length in two recent texts devoted to this all-important concern with generalization and endurance of treatment effects (Goldstein & Kanfer, 1979; Karoly & Steffen, 1980).

A thorough review of psychotherapy outcome and follow-up research conducted by us (Goldstein & Stein, 1976) revealed that "though the number of studies reporting positive therapeutic outcomes is high (85%), only 14% of the studies conducted report maintenance or transfer of therapeutic gains" (Goldstein & Kanfer, 1979, p. 2). This exceedingly low level of persistence of effect has also been documented by many others (e.g., Kazdin, 1975; Keeley, Shemberg & Carbonell, 1976; Margolin, Siegel, & Phillips, 1976). It is to be noted and underscored in this context, however, that in our research on Structured Learning we have been able to attain a skill transfer effect in approximately 45 to 50% of the trainees involved. This skill transfer effect appears to occur in direct proportion to the number of specific transfer-enhancing procedures (see Table 1) explicitly incorporated into the Structured Learning format.

DEALING WITH MANAGEMENT PROBLEMS AND RESISTIVE BEHAVIOR

In Structured Learning groups, as in all training or psychotherapy interventions, group members may actively resist participation as prescribed (e.g., cutting, lateness, refusal to role play, walking out), may participate but inappropriately (e.g., excessive restlessness, inattention, inability to remember procedures), display one or another form of inactivity (e.g., apathy, minimal participation, falling asleep), or hyperactivity (interrupting, monopolizing, digressing, jumping out of role). To deal effectively and rapidly with this array of group or individual management problems, we utilize one or more of the following resistance-reducing techniques:

1. *Empathic encouragement.* This intervention consists of: (a) offering the trainee the opportunity to explain in greater detail his/her difficulty in participating as instructed and listening nondefensively; (b) clearly expressing your understanding of the trainee's feelings; (c) if appropriate, responding that the trainee's view is a viable alternative; (d) presenting your own view in greater detail with both supporting reasons and probable outcomes; (e) expressing the appropriateness of delaying a resolution of the trainee-trainer difference; and (f) urging the trainee to tentatively try to participate.

2. *Reinstruct and simplify.* This approach may be implemented in one or more of the following ways: (a) Have the trainee follow one behavioral step, rather than a series of steps. (b) Have the trainee play a passive (co-actor or nonspeaking) role in the role play prior to playing the role of the main actor. (c) Cut the role play short. (d) Instruct the trainee in what to say in the role play (either prior to the role play or in a coaching fashion during the role play). (e) Reinforce the trainee for improvement over prior performance rather than having him/her live up to standards set for other members.

3. *Reduce threat.* For trainees who find some aspect of the Structured Learning session threatening or anxiety-producing, we recommend a series of procedures designed to help the trainee calm down sufficiently so that he/she can attend to the task at hand. Some threat reduction methods include: (a) Have one of the trainers

model a particular task before asking the threatened trainee to try the task. (b) Reassure the trainee with remarks such as "Take your time," "I know it's hard," or "Give it a try and I'll help you through it." (c) Clarify any aspects of the trainee's task which are still unclear.

4. Elicit responses. This set of methods is called for in cases where the group is being unresponsive to efforts to get trainees involved. Some elicitation methods include: (a) Call for volunteers. (b) Introduce topics for discussion. (c) Ask a specific trainee to participate, preferably someone who has shown some signs of interest or attention (i.e., eye contact, gesture).

5. Terminate responses. Finally, urge trainers to take a direct stand in situations which divert the attention of the group from the task at hand. Some termination methods include: (a) Interrupt ongoing behavior. (b) Extinguish through inattention to trainee behavior. (c) Cease interaction with resistive trainee and ask others to participate. (d) Urge trainees to get back on the correct topic.

RESEARCH EVALUATION

Starting in 1970, our research group has conducted a systematic research program oriented toward evaluating and improving the effectiveness of Structured Learning. Approximately 50 investigations have been conducted involving a wide variety of trainee populations. These include chronic adult schizophrenics (Goldstein, 1973; Goldstein, Sprafkin & Gershaw, 1976, 1979; Liberman, 1970; Orenstein, 1969; Sutton-Simon, 1974), geriatric patients (Lopez, 1977; Lopez, Hoyer, Goldstein, Gershaw, & Sprafkin, 1980), child abusing parents (Solomon, 1977; Sturm, 1980), young children (Hummel, 1980; Swanstrom, 1974), such change-agent trainees as mental hospital staff (Berlin, 1974; Goldstein & Goodhart, 1973; Lack, 1975; Robinson, 1973; Schneiman, 1972), police (Goldstein, Monti, Sardino, & Green, 1979), persons employed in industrial contexts (Goldstein & Sorcher, 1973, 1974), and in recent years aggressive and other behaviorally disordered adolescents (Goldstein, Sprafkin, Gershaw, & Klein, 1979,1980; Greenleaf, 1980; Litwack, 1976; Trief, 1976; Wood, 1977).

With regard to adolescent trainees, Structured Learning has been successful in enhancing such prosocial skills as empathy, negotiation, assertiveness, following instructions, self-control, and perspective taking. Beyond these initial demonstrations that Structured Learning *works* with youngsters, these beginning studies have also highlighted other aspects of the teaching of prosocial behaviors. Fleming (1976), in an effort to capitalize upon adolescent responsiveness to peer influence, demonstrated that gains in negotiating skill are as great when the Structured Learning group leader is a respected peer as when the leader is an adult. Litwack (1976), more concerned with the skill-enhancing effects of an adolescent anticipating that he will later serve as a peer leader, showed that such helper role expectation increases the degree of skill acquired. Apparently, when the adolescent expects to teach others a skill, his own level of skill acquisition benefits, a finding clearly relevant to Reissman's helper therapy principle (1965). Trief (1976) demonstrated that successful use of Structured Learning to increase the perspective-taking skill (i.e., seeing matters from other people's viewpoint) also leads to consequent increases in cooperative behavior. The significant transfer effects both in this study and in the Golden (1975), Litwack (1976), and Raleigh (1977) investigations have been

Structured Learning has been successful in enhancing prosocial skills with adolescent students.

> Aggression-prone adolescents often get into difficulty when they respond with overt aggression to authority figures with whom they disagree.

important signposts in planning further research on transfer enhancement in Structured Learning.

As in earlier efforts with adult trainees, the value of teaching certain skill combinations has begun to be examined. Aggression-prone adolescents often get into difficulty when they respond with overt aggression to authority figures with whom they disagree. Golden (1975), responding to this type of event, successfully used Structured Learning to teach such youngsters *resistance-reducing behavior*, defined as a combination of reflection of feeling (the authority figure's) and assertiveness (forthright but nonaggressive statement of one's own position). Jennings (1975) was able to use Structured Learning successfully to train adolescents in several of the verbal skills necessary for satisfactory participation in more traditional, insight-oriented psychotherapy. And Guzzetta (1974) was successful in providing means to help close the gap between adolescents and their parents by using Structured Learning to teach empathic skills to parents.

The overall conclusions which may justifiably be drawn from these several empirical evaluations of our work with adolescent as well as other trainees are threefold.

1. Skill acquisition. Across diverse trainee populations (clearly including aggressive adolescents in urban secondary schools and juvenile detention centers) and target skills, skill acquisition is a reliable training outcome, occurring in well over 90% of Structured Learning trainees. While pleased with this outcome, we are acutely aware of the manner in which therapeutic gains demonstrable *in the training context* are rather easily accomplished—given the potency, support, encouragement, and low-threat value of trainers and therapists in that context—but that the more consequential outcome question by far pertains to trainee skill performance *in real-world contexts* (i.e., skill transfer).

2. Skill transfer. Across diverse trainee populations, target skills, and applied (real-world) settings, skill transfer occurs with approximately 50% of Structured Learning trainees. Goldstein and Kanfer (1979) as well as Karoly and Steffen (1980) have indicated that across several dozen types of psychotherapy involving many different types of psychopathology, the average transfer rate on follow-up is between 15% and 20% of patients seen. The 50% rate consequent to Structured Learning is a significant improvement upon this collective base rate, though it must immediately be underscored that this cumulative average transfer finding also means that the gains shown by half of our trainees were limited to insession acquisition. Of special consequence, however, is the consistently clear manner in which skill transfer in our studies was a function of the explicit implementation of laboratory derived transfer-enhancing techniques, such as those described earlier in this article.

3. Prescriptiveness. A prescriptive research strategy is, at heart, an effort to conceptualize, operationalize, and evaluate potentially optimal trainer x trainee x training method matches. Prior to constituting such combinations, trainer, trainee, and training characteristics which may be active contributors to such matches must be examined singly and in combination. Stated otherwise, active and inert contributors to skill acquisition and transfer must be identified. A small and continuing series of multiple regression investigations conducted by us have begun to point to state, trait, cognitive, demographic, and sociometric predictors of high levels of skill acquisition and transfer (Anderson, 1981; Hoyer, Lopez, &

Goldstein, 1982). More such prescriptive ingredients research seems worthy of pursuit.

REFERENCES

Agras, W. S. (1967). Transfer during systematic desensitization therapy. *Behavior Research and Therapy, 5,* 193-199.

Anderson, L. (1981). *Role playing ability and young children: The prescriptive question.* Unpublished masters thesis, Syracuse University.

Authier, J., Gustafson, K., Guerney, B. G., Jr., & Kasdorf, J. A. (1975). The psychological practitioner as teacher. *The Counseling Psychologist, 5,* 1-21.

Berlin, R. J. (1974). *Training of hospital staff in accurate effective perception fear-anxiety from vocal cues in the context of varying facial cues.* Unpublished masters thesis, Syracuse University.

Callantine, M. F., & Warren, J. M. (1955). Learning sets in human concept formation. *Psychological Reports, 1,* 363-367.

Cartledge, G., & Milburn, J. (1978). The case for teaching social skills in classroom: A review. *Review of Educational Research, 48*(11), 133-156.

Cartledge, G., & Milburn, J. (1980). *Teaching social skills to children.* New York: Pergamon Press.

Chapman, W. E. (1977). *Roots of character education.* Schenectady, NY: Character Research Press.

Dewey, J. (1938). *Experience and Education.* New York: Collier.

Duncan, C. P. (1959). Recent research on human problem solving. *Psychological Bulletin, 56,* 397-429.

Ellis, H. (1965). *The transfer of learning.* New York: Macmillan.

Fleming, D. (1976). *Teaching negotiation skills to pre-adolescents.* Unpublished doctoral dissertation, Syracuse University.

Golden, R. (1975). *Teaching resistance-reducing behavior to high school students.* Unpublished doctoral dissertation, Syracuse University.

Goldstein, A. P. (1973). *Structured learning therapy. Toward a psychotherapy for the poor.* New York: Academic Press.

Goldstein, A. P. (1981). *Psychological skill training.* New York: Pergamon Press.

Goldstein, A. P., & Goedhart, A. (1973). The use of structured learning for empathy-enhancement in paraprofessional psychotherapist training. *Journal of Community Psychology, 1,* 168-173.

Goldstein, A. P., and Kanfer, F. (Eds.). (1979). *Maximizing treatment gains.* New York: Academic Press.

Goldstein, A. P., Monti, P. J., Sardino, T. J., & Green, D. J. (1979). *Police crisis intervention.* New York: Pergamon Press.

Goldstein, A. P., & Sorcher, M. (1973, March). Changing managerial behavior by applied learning techniques. *Training & Development Journal,* 36-39.

Goldstein, A. P., & Sorcher, M. (1974). *Changing supervisor behavior.* New York: Pergamon Press.

Goldstein, A. P., Sprafkin, R. P., & Gershaw, N. J. (1976). *Skill training for community living.* New York: Pergamon Press.

Goldstein, A. P., Sprafkin, R. P., & Gershaw, N.J. (1979). *I know what's wrong, but I don't know what to do about it.* Englewood Cliffs, NJ: Spectrum.

Goldstein, A. P., Sprafkin, R. P., Gershaw, N. J., & Klein, P. (1979). *Skill streaming the adolescent.* Urbana, IL: Research Press.

Goldstein, A. P., Sprafkin, R. P., Gershaw, N. J., & Klein, P. (1980). Structured learning and the skill deficient adolescent. In G. Carteledge & J. Milburn (Eds.), *Teaching social skills to children.* New York: Pergamon Press.

Goldstein, A. P., & Stein, N. (1976). *Prescriptive psychotherapies.* New York: Pergamon Press.

Greenleaf, D. (1977). *Peer reinforcement as transfer enhancement in structured learning therapy.* Unpublished masters thesis, Syracuse University.

Gruber, R. P. (1971). Behavior therapy: Problems in generalization. *Behavior Therapy, 2,* 361-368.

Gutride, M. E., Goldstein, A. P., & Hunter, G. F. (1973), The use of modeling and role playing to increase social interaction among asocial psychiatric patients. *Journal of Consulting and Clinical Psychology, 40,* 408-415.

Guzzetta, R. A. (1974). *Acquisition and*

transfer of empathy by the parents of early adolescents through structured learning training.* Unpublished doctoral dissertation, Syracuse University.

Hoyer, W. J., Lopez, M., & Goldstein, A. P. (1982). Predicting social skill acquisition and transfer by psychogeriatric inpatients. *International Journal of Behavioral Geriatrics, 1,* 43-46.

Hummel, J. W. (1980). *An examination of structured learning therapy, self-control, negotiations training, and variations in stimulus conditions.* Unpublished doctoral dissertation, Syracuse University.

Jennings, R. L. (1975). *The use of structured learning techniques to teach attraction enhancing interviewee skills to residentially hospitalized lower socioeconomic, emotionally disturbed children and adolescents: A psychotherapy analogue investigation.* Unpublished doctoral dissertation, University of Iowa.

Karoly, P., & Steffen, J. J. (Eds.). (1980). *Improving the long-term effects of psychotherapy.* New York: Gardner Press.

Kazdin, A. E. (1975). *Behavior modification in applied settings.* Homewood, IL: Dorsey Press.

Keeley, S. M., Shemberg, K. M., & Carbonell, J. (1976). Operant clinical intervention: Behavior management or beyond? *Behavior Therapy, 7,* 292-305.

Kohlberg, L. (1973). *Collected papers on moral development and moral education.* Cambridge, MA: Harvard Graduate School of Education.

Lack, D. Z. (1975). *Problem-solving training, structured learning training, and didactic instruction in the preparation of paraprofessional mental health personnel for the utilization of contingency management techniques.* Unpublished doctoral dissertation, Syracuse University.

Larsen, D. (in press). *Giving psychology away.* San Francisco: Brooks Cole.

Liberman, B. (1970). *The effect of modeling procedures on attraction and disclosure in a psychotherapy analogue.* Unpublished doctoral dissertation, Syracuse University.

Litwack, S. E. (1977). *The use of the helper therapy principle to increase therapeutic effectiveness and reduce therapeutic resistance: Structured learning therapy with resistant adolescents.* Unpublished doctoral dissertation, Syracuse University.

Lopez, M. (1977). *The effects of overlearning and prestructuring in structured learning therapy with geriatric patients.* Unpublished doctoral dissertation, Syracuse University.

Lopez, M. A., Hoyer, W. J., Goldstein, A. P., Gershaw, N. J., & Sprafkin, R. P. (1980). Effects of overlearning and incentive on the acquisition and transfer of interpersonal skills with institutionalized elderly, *Journal of Gerontology, 35*(3), 403-408.

Marholin, D., Siegel, L. J., & Phillips, D. (1976). Treatment and transfer: A search for empirical procedures. In M. Hersen, R. M. Eisler, & P. M. Miller (Eds.), *Progress in behavior modification* (Vol. 3). New York: Academic Press.

Miller, J. P. (1976). *Humanizing the classroom.* New York: Praeger.

Orenstein, R. (1969). The influence of self-esteem on modeling behavior in a psychotherapy analogue. Unpublished masters thesis, Syracuse University.

Osgood, C. E. (1953). *Method and theory in experimental psychology.* New York: Oxford University Press.

Patterson, G. R., & Gullion, M. E. (1972). *Living with children.* Champaign, IL: Research Press.

Raleigh, R. (1977). *Individual vs. group-structured learning therapy for assertiveness training with senior and junior high school students.* Unpublished doctoral dissertation, Syracuse University.

Rathjen, D., & Foreyt, J. (1980). *Social competence: Intervention for children and adults.* New York: Pergamon Press.

Reissman, F. (1965). *The culturally deprived child.* New York: Harper.

Robinson, R. (1973). *Evaluation of a structured learning empathy training program for lower socioeconomic status home-aide trainees.* Unpublished masters thesis, Syracuse University.

Schneiman, R. (1972). *An evaluation of structured learning and didactic learning as methods of training behaviormodification skills to lower and middle socioeconomic level teacher-aides.* Unpublished doctoral dissertation, Syracuse University.

Shore, E., & Sechrest, L. (1961). Concept attainment as a function of number of positive instances presented. *Journal of Educational Psychology, 52,* 303-307.

Simon, S. B., Howe, L. W., & Kirschenbaum, H. (1972). *Values clarification.* New York: Hart.

Solomon, E. (1978). *Structured learning therapy with abusive parents: Training in self-control.* Unpublished doctoral dissertation, Syracuse University.

Swanstron, C. (1974). *Training self-control in behavior problem children.* Unpublished doctoral dissertation, Syracuse University.

Sturm, D. (1980). *Therapist aggression tolerance and dependency tolerance under standardized client conditions of hostility and dependency.* Unpublished masters thesis, Syracuse University.

Tharp, R. G., & Wetzel, R. (1969). *Behavior modification in the natural environment.* New York: Academic Press.

Thorndike, E. L., & Woodworth, R. S. (1901). The influence of improvement in one mental function upon the efficiency of other functions. *Psychological Review, 8,* 247-261.

Trief, P. (1976). *The reduction of egocentrism in acting-out adolescents by structured learning therapy.* Unpublished doctoral dissertation, Syracuse University.

Weinstein, G., & Fantini, M. D. (1970). *Toward humanizing education: A curriculum of affect.* New York: Praeger.

Wood, M. (1977). *Adolescent acquisition and transfer of assertiveness through the use of structured learning therapy.* Unpublished doctoral dissertation, Syracuse University.

Use of Cognitive Mediation Strategies for Social Skills Training: Theoretical and Conceptual Issues

John W. Maag

ABSTRACT: Social skills training curricula have been used to teach appropriate social interaction to behaviorally disordered youth. Concomitantly, cognitive interventions such as self-management training have been advocated for enhancing generalization and maintenance of treatment effects. The purpose of this article is to discuss the benefits of incorporating cognitive mediation strategies into social skills training interventions. Cognitive mediation techniques are described and relevant literature reviewed. Issues related to treatment implementation of cognitive mediation strategies for social skills training are discussed.

Reprinted from *Monograph in Behavioral Disorders, Volume 12,* Summer 1989, pp. 87-100

Development of social skills training procedures have burgeoned during the past decade. Standardized empirically-based curricula and materials are readily available to clinicians and educators (cf. McConnell, 1987). Despite advances in applied social skills technology, prospects for generalization and maintenance of trained social skills remain dismal (Schloss, Schloss, Wood, & Kiehl, 1986). While considerable information exists for programming generalization (e.g., Stokes & Baer, 1977), and while it is discussed by authors of social skills training curricula (e.g., Goldstein, Sprafkin, Gershaw, & Klein, 1980; Walker et al., 1983), seldom are generalization procedures systematically incorporated into social skills treatment efficacy studies (Schloss et al., 1986).

Stokes and Osnes (1986, 1988) recently described 11 tactics for promoting the successful programming of generalization. These tactics may be roughly classified into two general categories: environmental manipulation and cognitive mediation (Maag, in press). Environmental manipulation techniques such as the use of multiple peer exemplars, structuring interaction with significant others, integrating training into natural environments (Shores, 1987), and in particular, promoting entrapment effects (McConnell, 1987) have been proffered as efficient generalization enhancers. Unfortunately, several methodological problems limit the efficacy of solely relying on environmental manipulation techniques for promoting generalization of social skills. The concept of entrapment provides an excellent example of two of these drawbacks.

> In order for entrapment to occur, the student's trained social skill(s) must be reinforced by their peers and vice-versa, thereby perpetuating positive reciprocal interaction.

Entrapment refers to a bidirectional reciprocal process whereby newly acquired behaviors are maintained by naturally occurring communities of social reinforcers (McConnell, 1987). It reflects a shift in stimulus control from training to generalization settings. In order for entrapment to occur, the student's trained social skill(s) must be reinforced by their peers and vice-versa, thereby perpetuating positive reciprocal interaction. Unfortunately, it is unlikely that appropriate social responses always can come under the control of naturally occurring reinforcers. There are many instances when appropriate behaviors are not reinforced by others. For example, employers often fail to praise employees for exemplary work, or students exhibiting appropriate group entry skills frequently are shunned by their peers. More problematic has been indications that even when rejected students engage in prosocial behaviors, they continue to be rejected by their peers (Bierman & Furman, 1984; Bierman, Miller, & Stabb, 1987). The elusive goal of improved peer acceptance following social skills training threatens the theoretical underpinnings of entrapment for promoting generalization. It is unlikely that reciprocity of reinforcement will occur if a student's peer group continues to dislike him or her after demonstrating improved social skills.

Despite the success of operant procedures for teaching social skills, several researchers have advocated the use of cognitive mediation strategies for promoting generalization because of their reduced reliance upon environmental contingencies to maintain behaviors in nontreatment settings (e.g., Gross & Drabman, 1982; Kanfer & Karoly, 1982; Kendall & Braswell, 1982). Cognitive mediation represents a fairly new area of social skills training research when compared to the attention environmental manipulation strategies receive (Simpson, 1987). Currently, there is a need to systematically investigate the differential efficacy of cognitive mediation strategies for social skills training interventions (Meador & Ollendick, 1984).

The purpose of this article is to discuss the benefits of cognitive mediation strategies for social skills training interventions. Several cognitive mediation strategies will be described and relevant research discussed for (a) self-instruction training, (b) self-management training, (c) problem-solving training, (d) attribution retraining, and (e) relaxation training. Issues related to treatment implementation are discussed. This article is intended to present a theoretical and conceptual framework for future research and application of cognitive mediation strategies for social skills training.

COGNITIVE MEDIATION STRATEGIES

Cognitive mediation strategists attempt to place the responsibility for change or skill acquisition/production on the individual. The self-regulatory nature of cognitive mediation has resulted in maintenance and generalization of behavior change in some students exhibiting maladaptive behavior (e.g., Kendall & Braswell, 1982; Lochman & Lampron, 1988). Although methodological deficiencies using cognitive mediation strategies with children have been noted on such variables as subject selection, adequacy of outcome measures, and experimental and statistical methodology (Hobbs, Moguin, Tyroler, & Lahey, 1980), a growing number of researchers reported promising results that merit further investigation. However, two theoretical issues should be addressed which have procedural implications for application of these treatment techniques.

First, practitioners should take into consideration the similarity and overlap among many cognitive mediation strategies. All cognitive mediation techniques involve self-instruction or private speech. For example, individuals engage in self-instruction or private speech when self-monitoring, self-evaluating, and administering self-reinforcement/punishment by deciding when and what behavior they should emit, if the behavior is performed appropriately, and what type of self-reinforcement/punishment they deserve. Similarly, in order to employ relaxation training, individuals must use self-instructions for determining situations that require the relaxation response and for performing the response correctly. Problem-solving training probably represents the most inclusive and systematic use of self-instructions. Braswell and Kendall (1988) suggested that a problem-solving approach to behavioral or interpersonal dilemmas represents the general orientation of cognitive-behavioral interventions.

Second, it is important for practitioners to preserve an environmental/behavioral view of treatment. Social interaction requires individuals to function within the social context (Kendall, 1985). This view is reflected by the importance given to structuring environmental conditions (e.g., entrapment) to promote generalized social interaction skills (Gaylord-Ross & Haring, 1987). As promising as environmental manipulation techniques appear, it is not possible nor desirable to structure all social contexts to become conducive for social reciprocity occurring. However, individuals can be taught cognitive mediation strategies to use regardless of the social context and environmental demands of a given situation.

Self-Instruction Training

Verbal mediation, private speech, and self-instruction are synonymous terms for a person making covert or overt mediated responses when presented with a learning task. Teaching students self-instruction tactics has been effective in training (a) behaviorally disordered children to increase attending and on-task behaviors (Barkley, Copeland, & Sivage, 1980; Bornstein & Quevillon, 1976; Kendall & Braswell, 1982; Kendall & Wilcox, 1980; Kendall & Zupan, 1981; Morrow & Morrow, 1985); (b) increasing academic skills (Bryant & Budd, 1982; Graham, 1983; Harris, 1986a; Leon & Pepe, 1983); and (c) increasing appropriate social behaviors (Burron & Bucher, 1978; Kneedler, 1980).

Host studies investigating the use of self-instruction have used adaptations of a training sequence developed by Meichenbaum and Goodman (1971): *(a) cognitive modeling*—an adult model performs a task while talking to himself out loud; (b) *overt, external guidance*—the student performs the same task under the direction of the model's instructions; (c) *overt, self-guidance*—the student performs the task while instructing himself aloud; (d) *faded, overt self-guidance*—the student whispers the instructions to himself while going through the task; and (e) *covert self-instruction*—the student performs the task while guiding his performance via private speech (p. 32). This method has been commonly referred to as the "faded rehearsal" method of self-instruction training. A modification of this approach which has become more popular in recent years is the "directed discovery" method. In the latter method, the trainer leads the student to *discover* specific sets of self-guiding strategies through Socratic dialogue rather than providing the student with predetermined strategies (Braswell & Kendall, 1988).

Self-Management Training

Self-management training involves the personal application of tech-

> Cognitive mediation strategists attempt to place the responsibility for change or skill acquisition/production on the individual.

> As an isolated procedure, self-evaluation has not been particularly effective for reducing disruptive classroom behaviors nor for strengthening appropriate behaviors.

niques for individuals changing their own behavior. Self-management training usually involves self-monitoring, self-evaluation, self-determination of contingencies, and self-instruction (cf. O'Leary & Dubey, 1979; Rosenbaum & Drabman, 1979). The focus of this section will be on the first three techniques as self-instruction was addressed previously. Although self-management training has been used for promoting generalized behavior change (Baer, Holman, Stokes, Fowler, & Rowbury, 1981) and improving academic skills (Harris & Graham, 1985), few researchers have employed simultaneously all four techniques in treatment efficacy studies. Rather, individual techniques have become major therapeutic interventions in their own right.

Self-Monitoring. Self-monitoring has been defined as an individual's systematic observation of her/his own behavior and recording a specified target response (Cooper, Heron, & Heward, 1987). Self-monitoring has been used successfully to increase students' attention in the classroom (Broden, Hall, & Mitts, 1971; Kneedler & Hallahan, 1981), decrease disruptive behaviors (Lovitt, 1973; Stevenson & Fantuzzo, 1984; Sugai & Rowe, 1984), and improve academic performance (Harris, 1986b; Hundert & Bucher, 1978; James, Trap, & Cooper, 1977).

Self-monitoring can have a reactive effect on the target response being self-observed, whereby the behavior changes as a function of the self-monitoring process (Rosenbaum & Drabman, 1979). Thus, the act of engaging in self-observation can be an effective behavior change technique. Self-monitoring has been suggested to result in behavior change because it produces positive or negative self-evaluative statements that serve to either reinforce desirable behaviors or to punish undesirable behaviors (Cautela, 1971; Malott, 1981).

Self-Evaluation. The distinction between self-monitoring and self-evaluation often is arbitrary. For example, if self-monitoring is to result in behavior change, it must be accompanied by self-evaluative statements. However, O'Leary and O'Leary (1976) distinguished between self-monitoring and self-evaluation. Although both procedures entail self-observation, in self-monitoring behavior is monitored and recorded with a minimum amount of judgment. In self-evaluation, the self-monitoring process is followed by a covert evaluation of the behavior, usually with an externally provided criterion. Therefore, self-evaluation is a necessary component for self-monitoring to result in behavior change.

Several researchers attempted to isolate the effects of self-evaluation from self-monitoring. As an isolated procedure, self-evaluation has not been particularly effective for reducing disruptive classroom behaviors (Santogrossi, O'Leary, Romanczyk, & Kaufman, 1973; Turkewitz, O'Leary, & Ironsmith, 1975) nor for strengthening appropriate behaviors (Layne, Rickard, Jones, & Lyman, 1976). Although some success has been demonstrated with self-evaluation procedures (e.g., Nelson, Lipinski, & Boykin, 1978; Sagotsky, Patterson, & Lepper, 1978), O'Leary and Dubey (1979) suggested their effectiveness may be increased when used in combination with self-monitoring and reinforcement.

Self-Reinforcement/Punishment. Self-reinforcement/punishment involves arranging to have one's own behavior receive specified consequences according to self-planned contingencies of reinforcement and/or punishment (Cooper et al., 1987). It is difficult to evaluate effects of self-reinforcement procedures because of the confounding of self-monitoring, which is a necessary prerequisite to self-reinforcement. However, Masters and Santrock (1976) successfully isolated self-administered reinforcement from both self-monitoring and self-evaluation. Children who are taught to verbalize pride in their work demonstrated significantly greater task persistence than when they were told to utter neutral statements. Similarly, Ballard and Glynn (1975) found that while self-monitoring had no effect upon students' classroom writing skills, the sequential addition of self-reinforcement increased the accuracy and amount of writing skills.

Less research has been conducted on the effect of self-administered punishment. Self-determined response cost procedures have been used effectively for increasing students' social behavior (Kaufman & O'Leary, 1972) and academic work (Humphrey, Karoly, & Kirschenbaum, 1978). Contingent self-determined snaps of a rubberband (Mastellone, 1974) and timeout (James, 1981) have been used successfully to treat problematic behaviors. However, there is a clear trend for researchers and practitioners preferring to instruct youngsters in the use of self-reinforcement.

Problem-Solving Training

Problem-solving training represents a form of self-instruction for systematically approaching, evaluating, and solving interpersonal dilemmas (Braswell & Kendall, 1988). It depicts the general orientation of cognitive-behavioral methodology. Problem-solving interventions have been applied extensively with behaviorally disordered youngsters, For instance, Robin, Schneider, and Dolnick (1976) taught emotionally disturbed students to generate alternative solutions and examine their consequences to inhibit aggression and impulsivity in social situations. Amish, Gesten, Smith, Clark, and Stark (1988) trained behaviorally disordered children to generate significantly more alternative solutions to interpersonal problems than those generated by a control group of children. Problem-solving training also has been used successfully with delinquent and predelinquent adolescents (Sarason & Ganzer, 1973; Sarason & Sarason, 1981).

Lochman and colleagues developed an interpersonal cognitive problem-solving intervention for use with aggressive boys (cf. Lochman, Nelson, & Sims, 1981). Lochman, Burch, Curry, and Lampron (1984) and Lochman and Curry (1986) found that this problem-solving intervention plus a goal setting condition resulted in reductions in off-task passive behaviors, disruption, and aggression in the boys' classroom. Parent ratings of their child's aggression indicated some generalization of treatment effects to the home setting. Lochman and Lampron (1988) found that improvements in classroom behavior for aggressive boys receiving problem-solving training were maintained at a 7-month follow-up.

D'Zurilla (1988) suggested that social skills training programs should include training in problem-solving skills in order to enhance generalization of interpersonal skills. D'Zurilla (1986) described a five-component model for solving problems: (a) problem orientation, (b) problem definition and formulation, (c) generation of alternative solutions, (d) decision making, and (e) solution implementation and verification. In terms of clinical applications with children, Fischler and Kendall (1988) suggested that training programs should emphasize modeling and reinforcement of appropriate problem-solving strategies.

Problem-solving training represents a form of self-instruction for systematically approaching, evaluating, and solving interpersonal dilemmas and has been applied extensively with youngsters with behavioral disorders.

> The role of strategy selection is germane to the production of social skills.

Attribution Retraining

Attribution retraining arose from the viewpoint that children's causal explanations for why they are doing well or poorly has implications for their behavioral persistence, expectancies for future performance, and affective reactions to success and failure (Braswell & Kendall, 1988). Attribution retraining attempts to increase children's behavioral persistence on a task through use of effort-oriented statements. For example, Dweck (1975) found that when children who had difficulty solving math problems were instructed to tell themselves that "failure means you should try harder," they persisted longer on the problems than children in a success-only condition in which math problems were presented that were within their ability and that would ensure success.

Attributional beliefs also may affect students use of strategic behavior (Borkowski, Weyhing, & Turner, 1986). The role of strategy selection is germane to the production of social skills. Social skill deficits often can be traced to the inability of students to assemble and sequence subtasks into task strategies for successful performance (Harris, 1988; Howell, 1985). Kurtz and Borkowski (1984) found students who attributed success to effort were more likely to apply strategic behavior than students who attributed success to external factors. It appears likely that many motivational deficits in social skill knowledge and subsequent performance are linked to negative attributional states.

Before implementing attributional retraining for social skills training, two factors need to be considered. First, Pearl (1985) suggested that in order to be effective, attributional statements should be accompanied with specific behavioral efforts. For example, Short and Ryan (1984) found that attribution retraining was ineffective when students made effort-oriented statements prior to reading a passage rather than after having had difficulty with the passage. Second, Schunk (1983) suggested that attribution retraining is likely to be most successful with children who are not using the skills they possess. This approach would not be appropriate, for example, with children whose maladaptive behavior is due to specific skill deficits (Fincham, 1983).

Relaxation Training

Relaxation training techniques are designed to relieve distress and foster emotion-regulation (Meichenbaum, 1985). Emotion-regulation and cognitive mediation have been considered interrelated and inseparable concepts (Kendall, 1985; Santostefano & Reider, 1984). Progressive muscle relaxation has been the most widely used relaxation training technique with children. Muscle relaxation training has been used successfully to decrease disruptions and aggression and increase social skills and academic performance with behaviorally disordered, learning disabled, and mentally retarded students (Carter & Russell, 1980; Fejes & Prieto, 1987; Marholin, Steinman, Luiselli, Schwartz, & Townsend, 1979; Omizo, 1980; Robin et al., 1976; Walton, 1979).

Muscle relaxation generally involves having students tense and relax muscle parts of their bodies while focusing on how pleasant specific parts of the body feel when relaxed (cf. Jacobsen, 1938). This procedure is repeated with arms, legs, feet, hands, face, and stomach. After relaxation responses are practiced separately, they are incorporated into one motion. The whole body is tensed for a count of from one to 10 and then quickly relaxed.

Maag (1988a) suggested that progressive muscle relaxation provides a means for students to cope with situation-induced stress that otherwise may interfere with production of newly acquired social skills. In some instances, acquisition of social skills is mediated by the use of relaxation (Vallis, 1984). Practicing relaxation for social skills training is particularly germane when stressful or aversive situations can be neither altered nor avoided (Meichenbaum, 1985). Amerikaner and Summerlin (1982) found that teacher ratings of the acting out and distractibility of learning disabled students who received relaxation training were lower than for students who received social skills training. While this result should not be interpreted as support for the superiority of relaxation training over social skills training, it does point out the importance relaxation training plays in the amelioration of skill deficits.

THEORETICAL AND CONCEPTUAL TRAINING ISSUES

The rationale for incorporating cognitive mediation strategies into social skills training interventions largely evolved from Bandura's social learning theory. In particular, his research on modeling demonstrated that behavior is acquired through mediating influences of symbolic coding, cognitive organization, symbolic rehearsal, and motor rehearsal of information (Bandura, 1977, 1978). According to Bandura's conceptualization, environmental influences are "mediated" by cognitive processes. That is, a person's anticipation of reinforcing consequences (antecedent control) has a greater impact upon behavioral performance than the consequences on any particular response (consequent control; Gresham & Lemanek, 1983).

The strategies reviewed in this article focused upon the role of cognitive mediation in the acquisition and production of social skills. Although several researchers acknowledged the role of cognitive mediation for learning social skills (e.g., Craighead, 1982; Kazdin, 1982; Kendall & Braswell, 1982), few have systematically evaluated the efficacy of these strategies on actual performance of social skills. In fact, Gresham (1985) noted that while self-instruction and social problem-solving, for example, may represent effective social skills training strategies, little research has been conducted to demonstrate their effectiveness. Part of the difficulty in assessing efficacy of these strategies for social skills training is the absence of a comprehensive format for delivering training, inattention to conduct functional assessment, and inadequate implementation of tactics for promoting generalization. Each of these issues is discussed briefly within the context of cognitive mediation for social skills training.

Developing a Conceptual Model

The efficacy of cognitive mediation strategies for social skills training is interrelated to the conceptual model used to deliver treatment. Although there is an abundance of social skills training interventions (e.g., McConnell, 1987), Schloss et al. (1986) lamented that lack of a conceptual model for delivering training severely limits the ability to assess treatment efficacy. Having a structured training model is especially important for incorporating cognitive mediation strategies into social skills training programs. There is often an arbitrary distinction between behavioral and cognitive orientations. For instance, many cognitively-based strategies share behavioral methodology such as modeling, rehearsal, role playing, and instruction (Gresham, 1985; Maag, 1989).

> Research on modeling has demonstrated that behavior is acquired through mediating influences of symbolic coding, cognitive organization, symbolic rehearsal, and motor rehearsal of information.

> The multiplicity of social skills training techniques confounds the prospects for systematically delivering intervention in the absence of a structured conceptual model.

The multiplicity of social skills training techniques confounds the prospects for systematically delivering intervention in the absence of a structured conceptual model. The complexity and multifaceted nature of current social skills training programs is exemplified by Goldstein's (1988) PREPARE social curriculum. PREPARE includes ten courses encompassing a wide variety of behavioral and cognitive procedures: (a) interpersonal skills training; (b) anger control training; (c) moral reasoning training; (d) problem-solving training; (e) empathy training; (f) social perception training; (g) anxiety management; (h) cooperation training; (i) building a prosocial support group; and (j) understanding and using group processes. The first seven course offerings fall under the rubric of "cognitive" or "cognitive-behavioral" interventions.

This PREPARE curriculum represents diverse intervention strategies—each postulating slightly different theoretical orientations. Determining which technique(s) to employ first requires considerable skill conducting sophisticated multicomponent pretreatment assessment (Maag, in press). Assuming assessment yielded information regarding the reciprocal relationships among behavior, cognitions, and environment, implementing all or a combination of training techniques would be cumbersome and potentially overwhelming without having a conceptual training format from which to work.

A comprehensive training format would provide a structured system for employing various techniques that fall under the cognitive-behavioral rubric. One such conceptual format is offered in the stress inoculation training (SIT) paradigm. SIT has been used with behaviorally disordered youngsters to treat depression (Maag, 1988b), for aggression and anger management (Feindler & Fremouw, 1983; Maag, Parks, & Rutherford, 1989), and to teach interpersonal coping responses (Maag et al., 1989). Briefly, SIT consists of three phases: (a) *conceptualization*, (b) *skills acquisition and rehearsal*, and (c) *application and follow-through* (see Maag, 1988b, and Meichenbaum, 1985, for detailed description of stress inoculation training). SIT provides a structured format for assessing student and environmental characteristics, tailoring specific techniques to address assessment information, and providing in vitro and in vivo practice under conditions that arouse but do not overwhelm students' coping responses.

Functional Assessment

As interest in cognitive mediation strategies for social skills training grows, the need for assessing their differential efficacy also increases. Unfortunately, assessment methodology used in social skills training programs has been dismal. Criticisms include ignoring relationships between treatment techniques and specific subject characteristics, nonempirical methods of selecting target behaviors, failure to specify situational determinants of selected skills, and lack of using socially valid assessment measures (Gresham, 1985; Hughes & Sullivan, 1988; Schloss et al., 1986). All too often, students are taught to maintain eye contact, improve body posture, or increase question-asking without researchers or practitioners first determining whether students are actually deficient in these skills or whether intervention promotes socially important outcomes such as improved peer acceptance (Maag, in press).

The cavalier approach to social skills assessment often results from the need to operationalize behavior more precisely (Kazdin, 1985). Unfortunately, this practice ignores the fact that students' observed performance deficits may be due to (a) missing requisite behavioral skills, (b) inability to assemble and sequence subtasks into a task strategy for successful performance, (c) the selection of behaviors automatically rather than consciously, and (d) environmental antecedents and consequences militating against competent performance (Harris, 1985, 1988; Howell & Morehead, 1987; Long & Sherer, 1984).

In addition to problems in assessing individual-specific characteristics contributing to performance deficits and erroneous target behavior selection, few researchers have assessed the differential efficacy of specific training components—especially cognitive mediation strategies (Gresham, 1985). In order to determine their differential efficacy, cognitive mediation strategies must be selected to match specific student deficits as determined through pretraining assessment. It is clear that when training techniques are applied irrespective of assessment information, treatment efficacy is decreased (McKnight, Nelson, Hayes, & Jarrett, 1984). The ultimate benefit of cognitive mediation strategies for social skills training remains theoretically sound, but thus far requires considerable research.

Maintenance and Generalization

Perhaps no area of social skills training has generated as much attention as promoting generalization of behavior change. This area probably represents the biggest potential contribution cognitive mediation can offer for social skills training. In their seminal article, Stokes and Baer (1977) discussed the need to incorporate self-mediated stimuli into a program for promoting generalization. However, there continues to be a lack of programming for generalization in social skills training (e.g., Maag et al., 1989).

Perhaps the failure of researchers to implement effective generalization strategies in social skills training programs is due to the sophisticated nature of the process. Programming generalization requires time and practice and should be built into any serious social skills training program from its inception. Stokes and Osnes (1988) suggested that programming for generalization requires conducting functional assessment, yet relevant use of information gathered from this process often is omitted or ignored. To increase the understanding of generalization, generalization itself needs to be a major dependent variable, and generalization programming strategies need to be independent variables (Stokes & Osnes, 1988). Clearly, studying cognitive mediation strategies for social skills training needs to proceed on several fronts.

SUMMARY AND CONCLUSION

Cognitive mediation strategies have been proffered as a method for enhancing efficacy of social skills training interventions. Several of these strategies were reviewed including self-instruction training, self-management training, problem-solving training, attribution retraining, and relaxation training. Although these procedures have strong theoretical underpinnings, few researchers have assessed their differential efficacy for enhancing social skills training. Part of the difficulty has been the lack of a conceptual model from which to deliver treatment, inadequate or completely absent pretreatment assessment, and the lack of programming for generaliza-

---

No area of social skills training has generated as much attention as promoting generalization of behavior change.

tion. These issues must be addressed in order to substantiate the theoretical précis of cognitive mediation strategies for social skills training.

REFERENCES

Amerikaner, M., & Summerlin, M. L. (1982). Group counseling with learning disabled children: Effects of social skills and relaxation training on self-concept and classroom behavior. *Journal of Learning Disabilities, 15,* 340-343.

Amish, P. L., Gesten, E. L., Smith, J. K., Clark, H. B., & Stark, C. (1988). Social problem-solving training for severely emotionally and behaviorally disturbed children. *Behavioral Disorders, 13,* 175-186.

Baer, D. M., Holman, J., Stokes, T. F., Fowler, S. A., & Rowbury, T. G. (1981). Uses of self-control techniques in programming generalization. In S. W. Bijou & R. Ruiz (Eds.), *Behavior modification: Contributions to education* (pp. 39-61). Hillsdale, NJ: Lawrence Erlbaum.

Ballard, K. D., & Glynn, E. L. (1975). Behavioral self-management in story-writing with elementary school children. *Journal of Applied Behavior Analysis, 8,* 387-398.

Bandura, A. (1977). Self-efficacy: Toward a unifying theory of behavior change. *Psychological Review, 84,* 191-215.

Bandura, A. (1978). The self system in reciprocal determinism. *American Psychologist, 33,* 344-358.

Barkley, R., Copeland, A., & Sivage, C. (1980). A self-control classroom for hyperactive children. *Journal of Autism and Developmental Disorders, 10,* 75-89.

Bierman, K. L., & Furman, W. (1984). The effects of social skills training and peer involvement on the social adjustment of preadolescents. *Child Development, 55,* 151-162.

Bierman, K. L., Miller, C. L., & Stabb, S. D. (1987). Improving the social behavior and peer acceptance of rejected boys: Effects of social skill training with instructions and prohibitions. *Journal of Consulting and Clinical Psychology, 55,* 194-200.

Borkowski, J. G., Weyhing, R. S., & Turner, L. A. (1986). Attributional retraining and the teaching of strategies. *Exceptional Children, 53,* 130-137.

Bornstein, P. H., & Quevillon, R. P. (1976). The effects of a self-instructional package on overactive pre-school boys. *Journal of Applied Behavior Analysis, 9,* 179-188.

Braswell, L., & Kendall, P. C. (1988). Cognitive-behavioral methods with children. In K. S. Dobson (Ed.), *Handbook of cognitive-behavioral therapies* (pp. 167-213). New York: Guilford.

Broden, M., Hall, R. V., & Mitts, B. (1971). The effect of self-recording on the classroom behavior of two eighth-grade students. *Journal of Applied Behavior Analysis, 4,* 191-199.

Bryant, L. E., & Budd, K. S. (1982). Self-instructional training to increase independent work performance in preschoolers. *Journal of Applied Behavior Analysis, 15,* 259-271.

Burron, D., & Bucher, B. (1978). Self-instructions as discriminative cues for rule-breaking or rule-following. *Journal of Experimental Child Psychology, 26,* 46-57.

Carter, J. L., & Russell, H. L. (1980). Biofeedback and academic attainment of LD children. *Academic Therapy, 15,* 483-486.

Cautela, J. R. (1971). Covert conditioning. In A. Jacobs & L. B. Sachs (Eds.), *The psychology of private events: Perspective on covert response systems* (pp. 109-130). New York: Academic Press.

Cooper, J. O., Heron, T. E., & Heward, W. L. (1987). *Applied behavior analysis.* Columbus, OH: Merrill.

Craighead, W. E. (1982). A brief clinical history of cognitive-behavioral therapy with children. *School Psychology Review, 11,* 5-13.

Dweck, D. S. (1975). The role of expectations and attributions in the alteration of learned helplessness. *Journal of Personality and Social Psychology, 25,* 109-116.

D'Zurilla, T. J.,(1986). *Problem-solving therapy: A social competence approach to clinical interventions.* New York: Springer.

D'Zurilla, T. J. (1988). Problem-solving therapies. In K. S. Dobson (Ed.), *Handbook of cognitive-behavioral therapies* (pp. 85-135). New York: Guilford.

Feindler, E., & Fremouw, W. (1983). Stress inoculation training for adolescent anger problems. In D. Meichenbaum & M. Jaremko (Eds.), *Stress reduction and prevention* (pp. 451-485). New York: Plenum.

Fejes, K. E., & Prieto, A. G. (1987). The potential of relaxation training for the hyperkinetic trainable mentally retarded child. *Child and Family Behavior Therapy, 9,* 55-66.

Fincham, F. D. (1983). Clinical applications of attribution theory: Problems and prospects. In M. Hewstone (Ed.), *Attribution theory: Social and functional extensions* (pp. 187-203). Oxford: Blackwells.

Fischler, G. L., & Kendall, P. C. (1988). Social cognitive problem solving and childhood adjustment: Qualitative and topological analyses. *Cognitive Therapy and Research, 12,* 133-153.

Gaylord-Ross, R., & Haring, T. (1987). Social interaction research for adolescents with severe handicaps. *Behavioral Disorders, 12,* 264-275.

Goldstein, A. P. (1988). PREPARE: A prosocial curriculum for aggressive youth. In R. B. Rutherford, Jr., C. M. Nelson, & S. R. Forness (Eds.), *Bases of severe behavior disorders in children and youth* (pp. 119-142). San Diego, CA: College-Hill.

Goldstein, A. P., Sprafkin, R. P., Gershaw, N. J., & Klein, P. (1980). *Skill streaming the adolescent: A structured learning approach to teaching prosocial skills.* Champaign, IL: Research Press.

Graham, S. (1983). The effect of self-instructional procedures on LD students' handwriting performance. *Learning Disability Quarterly, 6,* 231-234.

Gresham, F. M. (1985). Utility of cognitive-behavioral procedures for social skill straining with children: A critical review. *Journal of Abnormal Child Psychology, 13,* 411-423.

Gresham, F. M., & Lemanek, K. L. (1983). Social skills: A review of cognitive-behavioral training procedures with children. *Journal of Applied Developmental Psychology, 4,* 239-261.

Gross, A. M., & Drabman, R. S. (1982). Teaching self-recording, self-evaluation, and self-reward to nonclinic children and adolescents. In P. Karoly & F. N. Kanfer (Eds.), *Self-management and behavior change; From theory to practice* (pp. 285-314). New York: Pergamon.

Harris, K. R. (1985). Conceptual, methodological, and clinical issues in cognitive-behavioral assessment. *Journal of Abnormal Child Psychology, 13,* 373-390.

Harris, K. R. (1986a). The effects of cognitive-behavior modification on private speech and task performance during problem solving among learning disabled and normally achieving children. *Journal of Abnormal Child Psychology, 14,* 63-67.

Harris, K. R. (1986b). Self-monitoring of attentional behavior versus self-monitoring of productivity: Effects on on-task behavior and academic response rate among learning disabled children. *Journal of Applied Behavior Analysis, 19,* 417-423.

Harris, K. R. (1988). Cognitive-behavior modification: Application with exceptional students. In E. L. Meyen, G. A. Vergason, & R. J. Whelan (Eds.), *Effective instructional strategies for exceptional children* (pp. 216-242). Denver: Love.

Harris, K. R., & Graham, S. (1985). Improving learning disabled students' composition skills: Self-control strategy training. *Learning Disabilities Quarterly, 8,* 27-36.

Hobbs, S. A., Moguin, L. E., Tyroler, M., & Lahey, B. B. (1980). Cognitive behavior therapy with children: Has clinical utility been demonstrated? *Psychological Bulletin, 87,* 147-165.

Howell, K. W. (1985). A task-analytic approach to social behavior. *Remedial and Special Education, 6,* 24-30.

Howell, K. W., & Morehead, M. K. (1987). *Curriculum-based evaluation for special and remedial education.* Columbus, OH: Merrill.

Hughes, J. S., & Sullivan, K. A. (1988). Outcome assessment in social skills training with children. *Journal of School Psychology, 26,* 167-183.

Humphrey, L. L., Karoly, P., & Kirschenbaum, D. S. (1978). Self-management in the classroom: Self-imposed response cost versus self-reward. *Behavior Therapy, 9,* 592-601.

Hundert, J., & Bucher, B. (1978). Pupils' self-scored arithmetic performance: A practical procedure for maintaining accuracy. *Journal of Applied Behavior Analysis, 11,* 304.

Jacobsen, E. (1938). *Progressive relaxation.* Chicago: University of Chicago Press.

James, J. C., Trap, J., & Cooper, J. O. (1977). Students' self-recording of manuscript letter strokes. *Journal of Applied Behavior Analysis, 10,* 509-514.

James, J. E. (1981). Behavioral self-control of stuttering using timeout from speaking. *Journal of Applied Behavior Analysis, 14,* 25-37.

Kanfer, F. N., & Karoly, P. (1982). The psychology of self-management: Abiding issues and tentative directions. In P. Karoly & F. N. Kanfer (Eds.), *Self-management and behavior change: From theory to practice* (pp. 571-599). New York: Pergamon.

Kaufman, K. F., & O'Leary, K. D. (1972). Reward, cost, and self-evaluation procedures for disruptive adolescents in a psychiatric hospital school. *Journal of Applied Behavior Analysis, 5,* 293-309.

Kazdin, A. E. (1982). Current developments and research issues in cognitive- behavioral interventions: A commentary. *School Psychology Review, 11,* 75-82.

Kazdin, A. E. (1985). Selection of target behaviors: The relationship of the treatment focus to clinical dysfunction. *Behavioral Assessment, 7,* 33-47.

Kendall, P. C. (1985). Toward a cognitive-behavioral model of child psychopathology and a critique of related interventions. *Journal of Abnormal Child Psychology, 13,* 357-372.

Kendall, P. C., & Braswell, L. (1982). Cognitive-behavioral self-control therapy for children: A components analysis. *Journal of Consulting and Clinical Psychology, 50,* 672-689.

Kendall, P. C., & Wilcox, L. E. (1980). A cognitive-behavioral treatment for impulsivity: Concrete versus conceptual training in non-self-controlled problem children. *Behavior Therapy, 12,* 344-359.

Kneedler, R. D. (1980). The use of cognitive training to change social behaviors. *Exceptional Education Quarterly, 1,* 65-73.

Kneedler, R. D., & Hallahan, D. P. (1981). Self-monitoring of on-task behavior with learning disabled children: Current studies and direction. *Exceptional Education Quarterly, 2*(3), 73-82.

Kurtz, B. E., & Borkowski, J. G. (1984). Children's metacognition: Exploring relations among knowledge, process, and motivational variables. *Journal of Experimental Child Psychology, 37,* 335-354.

Layne, C. C., Rickard, H. C., Jones, M. T., & Lyman, R. D. (1976). Accuracy of self-monitoring on a variable ratio schedule of observer verification. *Behavior Therapy, 7,* 481-488.

Leon, J. A., & Pepe, H. J. (1983). Self-instructional training: Cognitive behavior modification for remediating arithmetic deficits. *Exceptional Children, 50,* 54-60.

Lochman, J. E., Burch, P. R., Curry, J. F., & Lampron, L. B. (1984). Treatment and generalization effects of cognitive-behavioral and goal-setting interventions with aggressive boys. *Journal of Consulting and Clinical Psychology, 52,* 915-916.

Lochman, J. E., & Curry, J. F. (1986). Effects of social problem-solving training and self-instruction training with aggressive boys. *Journal of Clinical Child Psychology, 15,* 159-164.

Lochman, J. E., & Lampron, L. B. (1988). Cognitive-behavioral interventions for aggressive boys: 7-month follow-up effects. *Journal of Child and Adolescent Psychotherapy, 5,* 15-23.

Lochman, J. E., Nelson, W. M., III, & Sims, J. P. (1981). A cognitive behavioral program for use with aggressive children. *Journal of Clinical Child Psychology, 10,* 146-148.

Long, S. J., & Sherer, M. (1984). Social skills training with juvenile offenders. *Child and Family Behavior Therapy, 6,* 1-11.

Lovitt, T. C. (1973). Self-management projects with children with behavioral disabilities. *Journal of Learning Disabilities, 6,* 138-150.

Maag, J. W. (1988a). Palliative coping and social skills training: Guidelines and recommendations. *Perceptions, 24,* 32-33.

Maag, J. W. (1988b). Treatment of childhood and adolescent depression: Review and recommendation. In R. B. Rutherford, Jr., & J. W. Maag (Eds.), *Severe behavior disorders of children and youth* (Vol. 11, pp. 49-63). Reston, VA: Council for Children with Behavioral Disorders.

Maag, J. W. (1989). Moral discussion group interventions: Promising technique or wishful thinking? *Behavioral Disorders, 14,* 99-106.

Maag, J. W. (in press). Assessment in social skills training: Methodological and conceptual issues for research and practice. *Remedial and Special Education.*

Maag, J. W., Parks, B. T., & Rutherford, R. B., Jr. (1989). Generalization and behavior covariation of aggression in children receiving stress inoculation therapy. *Child and Family Behavior Therapy, 10,* 20-47.

Malott, R. W. (1981). *Notes from a radical behaviorist.* Kalamazoo, MI: Author.

Marholin, D., II, Steinman, W. M., Luiselli, J. K., Schwartz, C. S., & Townsend, N. M. (1979). The effects of progressive muscle relaxation on the behavior of autistic adolescents: A preliminary analysis. *Child Behavior Therapy, 1,* 75-84.

Mastellone, M. (1974). Aversion therapy: A new use of the old rubberband. *Journal of Behavior Therapy and Experimental Psychiatry, 5,* 311-312.

Masters, J. C., & Santrock, J. W. (1976). Studies in the self-regulation of behavior: Effects of contingent cognitive and affective events. *Developmental Psychology, 12,* 334-348.

McConnell, S. R. (1987). Entrapment effects and the generalization and maintenance of social skills training for elementary school students with behavioral disorders. *Behavioral Disorders, 12,* 252-263.

McKnight, D. L., Nelson, R. O., Hayes, S. C., & Jarrett, R. B. (1984). Importance of treating individually assessed response classes in the amelioration of depression. *Behavior Therapy, 15,* 315-335.

Meador, A. E., & Ollendick, T. H. (1984). Cognitive behavior therapy with children: An evaluation of its efficacy and clinical utility. *Child and Family Behavior Therapy, 6,* 25-44.

Meichenbaum, D. (1985). *Stress inoculation training.* New York: Pergamon.

Meichenbaum, D., & Goodman, J. (1971). Training impulsive children to talk to themselves: A means of developing self-control. *Journal of Abnormal Psychology, 77,* 115-126.

Morrow, L. W., & Morrow, S. A. (1985). Use of a verbal mediation procedure to reduce talking-out behaviors. In M. K. Zabel (Ed.), *TEACHING: Behaviorally disordered youth* (pp. 23-28). Reston, VA: Council for Children with Behavioral Disorders.

Nelson, R. O., Lipinski, D. P., & Boykin, R. A. (1978). The effects of self-recorders' training and the obtrusiveness of the self-recording of self-monitoring. *Behavior Therapy, 9,* 200-208.

O'Leary, S. G., & Dubey, D. R. (1979). Applications of self-control procedures by children: A review. *Journal of Applied Behavior Analysis, 12,* 449-475.

O'Leary, S. G., & O'Leary, K. D. (1976). Behavior modification in the school. In H. Leitenberg (Ed.), *Handbook of behavior modification and behavior therapy* (pp. 475-515). Englewood Cliffs, NJ: Prentice-Hall.

Omizo, M. M. (1980). The effects of biofeedback-induced relaxation training in hyperactive adolescent boys. *Journal of Psychology, 105,* 131-138.

Pearl, R. (1985). Cognitive-behavioral interventions for increasing motivation. *Journal of Abnormal Child Psychology, 13,* 443-454.

Robin, A. L., Schneider, M., & Dolnick, M. (1976). The turtle technique: An extended case of self-control in the classrooms. *Psychology in the Schools, 13,* 449-453.

Rosenbaum, M. S., & Drabman, R. S. (1979). Self-control training in the classroom: A review and critique. *Journal of Applied Behavior Analysis, 12,* 467-485.

Sagotsky, G., Patterson, C. J., & Lepper, M. R. (1978). Training children's self-control: A field experiment in self-monitoring and goal-setting in the classroom. *Journal of Experimental Child Psychology, 25,* 242-253.

Santogrossi, D. A., O'Leary, K. D., Romanczyk, R. G., & Kaufman, K. F. (1973). Self-evaluation by adolescents in a psychiatric hospital school token program. *Journal of Applied Behavior Analysis, 6,* 277-287.

Santostefano, S., & Reider, C. (1984). Cognitive controls and aggression in children. *Journal of Consulting and Clinical Psychology, 52,* 46-56.

Sarason, I. G., & Ganzer, V. J. (1973). Modeling and group discussion in the rehabilitation of juvenile delinquents. *Journal of Counseling Psychology, 20,* 442-449.

Sarason, I. G., & Sarason, B. R. (1981). Teaching cognitive and social skills to high school students. *Journal of Consulting and Clinical Psychology, 49,* 908-918.

Schloss, P. J., Schloss, C. N., Wood, C. E., & Kiehl, W. S. (1986). A critical review of social skills research with behaviorally disordered students. *Behavioral Disorders, 12,* 1-14.

Schunk, P. H. (1983). Ability versus effort attributional feedback: Differential effects on self-efficacy and achievement. *Journal of Educational Psychology, 75,* 848-856.

Shores, R. E. (1987). Overview of research on social interaction: A historical and personal perspective. *Behavioral Disorders, 12,* 233-241.

Short, E. J., & Ryan, E. B. (1984). Metacognitive differences between skilled and less skilled readers: Remediating deficits through story grammar and attribution training. *Journal of Educational Psychology, 76,* 225-235.

Simpson, R. L. (1987). Social interactions of behaviorally disordered children and youth: Where are we and where do we need to go? *Behavioral Disorders, 12,* 292-298.

Stevenson, H. C., & Fantuzzo, J. W. (1984). Application of the "generalization map" to a self-control intervention with schoolaged children. *Journal of Applied Behavior Analysis, 17,* 203-212.

Stokes, T. F., & Baer, D. M. (1977). An implicit technology of generalization. *Journal of Applied Behavior Analysis, 10,* 349-367.

Stokes, T. F., & Osnes, P. G. (1986). Programming the generalization of children's social behavior. In P. S. Strain, M. Guralnick, & H. Walker (Eds.), *Children's social behavior: Development, assessment, and modification* (pp. 407-443). Orlando, FL: Academic Press.

Stokes, T. F., & Osnes, P. G. (1988). The developing applied technology of generalization and maintenance. In R. H. Horner, G. Dunlap, & R. L. Koegel (Eds.), *Generalization and maintenance* (pp. 5-19). Baltimore, MD: Paul H. Brookes.

Sugai, G., & Rowe, P. (1984). The effect of self-recording on out-of-seat behavior of an EMR student. *Education and Training of the Mentally Retarded, 19,* 23-28.

Turkewitz, H. O'Leary, K. D., & Ironsmith, M. (1975). Generalization and maintenance of appropriate behavior through self-control. *Journal of Consulting and Clinical Psychology, 43,* 577-583.

Vallis, T. (1984). A complete component analysis of stress inoculation for pain tolerance. *Cognitive Therapy and Research, 8,* 313-330.

Walker, H. M., McConnell, S. R., Walker, J., Holmes, D., Todis, B., & Golden, N. (1983). *ACCEPTS: A curriculum for effect peer and teacher skills.* Austin, TX: Pro-Ed.

Walton, W. T. (1979). The use of a relaxation curriculum and biofeedback training in the classroom to reduce inappropriate behaviors of emotionally handicapped children. *Behavioral Disorders, 5,* 10-18.

Using a Peer Confrontation System in a Group Setting

Spencer J. Salend
Nancy Reid Jantzen
Karen Giek

ABSTRACT: The effectiveness of a peer confrontation system applied in a group setting was examined using a reversal design. Two groups of students with disabilities educated in a self-contained classroom within a public school program served as subjects for the study. The results show that a peer confrontation system was effective in modifying the inappropriate behavior of the two groups. Student satisfaction data indicate that the students had positive reactions to the system.

There has been a growing recognition of the value of using a variety of peer-mediated interventions to modify a wide range of classroom behaviors (Nelson, 1981; Salend, 1987; Smith & Fowler, 1984; Solomon & Wahler, 1973; Strain & Odom, 1986). One highly effective peer-mediated intervention is a peer confrontation system (Bellafiore & Salend, 1983; Sandler, Arnold, Gable, & Strain, 1987; Savicki, 1981). Peer confrontation is based on Vorrath and Brendtro's Positive Peer Culture Model (1974) which was developed to teach students to challenge the deviant behavior of their peers and to realize its effect on others. Peer confrontation employs a three-step model: (a) identifying the problem, (b) determining its effects on others, and (c) engaging in problem solving. Initially, peers identify the inappropriate behavior and challenge disruptive classmates to be aware of their behavior. Then, the peers discuss the consequences of the inappropriate behavior on others. Finally, peers engage in problem-solving to generate positive alternatives to the inappropriate behavior (Bellafiore & Salend, 1983; Candler & Goodman, 1979). Through problem-solving, peers are directly involved in helping classmates learn new behaviors while they in turn are learning appropriate responses to the disruptive behaviors of their classmates.

Peer confrontation also includes elements of mild punishment. Like a verbal reprimand such as *no*, the peer confrontation system may function as a conditioned aversive stimulus (Bellafiore & Salend, 1983; Greenwood & Hops, 1981). While research on the efficacy of verbal reprimands is mixed, several factors appear to contribute to the effectiveness of reprimands in the classroom (Van Houten, Nau, Mackenzie-Keating, Sameoto, & Calavecchia, 1982). These authors found that the effectiveness of reprimands was enhanced when the reprimand was (a) combined with nonverbal behaviors associated with reprimands (e.g., eye contact, firm

Reprinted from *Behavioral Disorders, Vol. 17, Number 3,* May 1992, pp. 211-218

> While the value of a peer confrontation system directed at individual students has appeared in the literature, there have been no studies to assess its effectiveness when applied to a group of students.

grasp), and (b) delivered in close proximity to the student. Using two same sex pairs of elementary level children, they also explored the effects of verbal reprimands directed at one member of the dyad during independent work time. In addition to reducing the inappropriate behavior of the reprimanded student, the verbal reprimands had positive spillover effects on the student sifting next to the reprimanded student.

Bellafiore and Salend (1983) illustrated that teacher-directed peer confrontation was a highly effective system for decreasing the inappropriate behavior of a targeted behaviorally disordered student. They also noted the intervention led to vicarious effects on the behavior of two nontargeted peers. Sandler et al. (1987) replicated these findings by demonstrating the effectiveness of the technique with middle school students with behavioral disorders. Lemlech (1979) and Savicki (1981) also reported using a peer confrontation system successfully.

While the value of a peer confrontation system directed at individual students has appeared in the literature (Bellafiore & Salend, 1983; Sandler et al., 1987), there have been no studies to assess its effectiveness when applied to a group of students. The present study was designed to investigate the efficacy of a peer confrontation system employed in a group setting. Additionally, data on the students' reactions to the system are presented.

METHOD

Subjects

Two groups of students with disabilities educated in a public school program served as subjects for this study. Students in both groups had been identified as having a disability by the school district's multidisciplinary team in accordance with New York state guidelines. The students received their academic program in a self-contained class and were integrated with their nonhandicapped peers for music, art, and physical education. Descriptive data on the students in this study are presented in Table 1.

Group A consisted of 9 males whose ages ranged from 8 years 7 months to 10 years 6 months. Of the students in Group A, 2 were classified as learning disabled, 4 were classified as emotionally disturbed, 2 were classified as mentally retarded, and 1 was classified as speech impaired. Their IQ scores as tested by the *Wechsler Intelligence Scale for Children Revised* (WISC-R; Wechsler, 1974) ranged from 61 to 106, with a mean of 88.

Group B consisted of 4 males and 1 female whose ages ranged from 8 years 5 months to 9 years 11 months. In Group B, 3 of the students were classified as learning disabled and 2 students were classified as emotionally disturbed. Their IQ scores as tested by the WISCR ranged from 81 to 105, with a mean of 93.

Setting

Data were collected during Group A's and Group B's language arts period. Group A's language arts period was conducted from 9:00 to 9:15 a.m., while Group B's language arts period occurred from 10:00 to 10:30 a.m. The length of these sessions remained consistent throughout the study. The instructional activities for Group A included oral reading and worksheets from the *Time Concept Series* (Dedrick & Lattyak, 1981), while Group B worked on spelling and language skills using the *Working Words in Spelling: Level B* (Woodruff & Moore, 1984) and *Language Skills: Level A* (Woodruff & Moore, 1987) programs.

TABLE 1
Descriptive Data on Students Across Groups

Student	Age	Sex	Disability*	IQ (WISC-R)	Woodcock-Johnson Percentile Scores Reading	Math
			Group A			
1	10-6	M	MH	61	0	0
2	9-1	M	MH	82	36	4
3	9-8	M	ED	106	6	16
4	8-7	M	ED	101	11	15
5	9-11	M	ED	94	13	24
6	8-11	M	SI	91	20	5
7	9-5	M	ED	78	8	8
8	9-11	M	LD	NA**	5	12
9	9-9	M	LD	91	19	11
			Group B			
1	9-8	M	ED	105	11	19
2	9-8	F	LD	81	1	9
3	9-11	M	LD	NA**	5	12
4	9-9	M	LD	91	19	11
5	8-5	M	ED	96	11	19

* MH = Mentally Handicapped, ED = Emotionally Disturbed, SI = Speech Impaired, LD = Learning Disabled

** NA = Not Available

> The teacher and teacher's aide selected the students' behaviors that were most disruptive and had the greatest negative impact on the learning environment.

Each group's language arts period took place in a classroom comprised of two standard-size classrooms separated by a sliding center divider that remained open throughout the study. The students and the teacher sat in chairs around the perimeter of two double-desks that were placed together. During this time period, the students were instructed by their language arts teacher who had undergraduate and master's degrees in special education and New York state certification in special education. At the time of this study, she had been teaching students with special education needs for 7 years.

Target Behaviors

The teacher and teacher's aide were asked to select the students' behaviors that were most disruptive and had the greatest negative impact on

> Data were collected by trained, independent observers, and interobserver agreement measures were obtained.

the learning environment. These inappropriate behaviors were then operationally defined and recorded during a pre-baseline period to assess their frequency. Those behaviors that occurred at high rates and were exhibited by several group members were selected as the target behaviors.

Because Group A's low levels of on-task behavior were interfering with instruction, the target behavior for Group A was to increase on-task behavior. On-task behavior was defined as eyes and/or pencil on the required book, workbook, paper, or assignment. It also included eyes on peers discussing the material and eyes on the teacher when instructions, directions, and feedback were given. On-task behavior also consisted of comments related to the material being covered in class.

Because the behavior that was considered most disruptive for Group B was inappropriate verbalizations, the target behavior for Group B was to decrease inappropriate verbalizations. Inappropriate verbalizations were defined as any student comment without teacher permission. Teacher permission could be granted by the teacher acknowledging a student's raised hand or the teacher requesting that a student respond verbally.

Data Recording Strategies

Data were collected by trained, independent observers. One observer was a graduate student working on obtaining her master's degree in special education. She had completed an undergraduate training program in special education and taught students with severe behavioral disorders for 2 years. The second observer was a community volunteer who had no formal training in special education.

The observers were trained using Salend's model (1983) for identifying and recording target behaviors over a 3-day period. Observer training consisted of reviewing, studying, and discussing the target behavior definitions and observation procedures. Next, observers viewed examples and nonexamples of the target behaviors and identified the salient features of the target behaviors. Observers also were asked to present examples of the target behavior. Finally, the observers role-played and practiced using the observation procedures.

Data on Group A's on-task behavior were collected by using a whole interval recording system of 15-sec intervals whereby students had to maintain on-task behavior throughout the entire interval. A whole interval recording system was employed because on-task behavior should be maintained for an extended period of time to be meaningful.

Event recording was employed to count the number of inappropriate verbalizations exhibited by Group B throughout the observation period because this behavior had discrete beginnings and endings. During Group B's language arts period, each time a student exhibited an inappropriate verbalization, it was recorded by the observer. If two students engaged in an inappropriate verbalization at the same time, two inappropriate verbalizations were recorded.

Interobserver Agreement

Interobserver agreement measures were obtained by having two trained observers independently record the target behaviors. For Group A, interobserver agreement measures on occurrence agreement were taken on 30% of the sessions and were distributed across all phases. Interobserver agreement was calculated by dividing the number of agreements by the number of agreements and disagreements on an interval by interval basis and multiplying by 100. Interobserver agreement measures had a mean of 84%. The mean interobserver agreement for Baseline 1, Intervention 1, Baseline 2, and Intervention 2 were 79, 86, 87, and 84%, respectively.

For Group B, interobserver agreement measures on occurrence agreement were taken on 28% of the sessions and were distributed across all phases. Since event recording was used to collect the data, interobserver agreement was calculated by dividing the smaller number of recorded inappropriate verbalizations by the larger for each observation and multiplying by 100. Interobserver agreement measures had a mean of 89%. The mean interobserver agreement for Baseline 1, Intervention 1, Baseline 2, and Intervention 2 were 81, 94, 82, and 95%, respectively.

Experimental Design

The study employed a reversal design (Baer, Wolf, & Risley, 1968). To help students discriminate baseline and treatment conditions, prior to each treatment session the teacher informed the students that "we will be using the system today" and then reviewed the system with them. Additionally, at the beginning of each Baseline 2 session, the students were told that "we are not going to use the system today." The procedures for evaluating the effectiveness of the intervention conditions are described below.

Baseline 1

Prior to instituting the peer confrontation system, data were collected on each group's target behavior. The teacher responded to the students' behavior in her usual manner. During baseline and throughout the study, the teacher implemented a classroom token system. Students earned tokens and received teacher praise at variable intervals for appropriate behaviors such as working quietly, staying in-seat, and completing their work. The number of tokens students earned during their language arts period depended upon each student's behavior. Typically, students earned between 3 and 8 tokens daily. At the end of the week, these tokens were exchanged for reinforcers such as magic markers, stickers, free time, books, and posters. Baseline 1 conditions were maintained for 7 days for both groups.

Intervention 1

The intervention was a teacher-directed peer confrontation system in which all group members participated. Each time a group member exhibited an inappropriate behavior (i.e., off-task behavior for Group A, inappropriate verbalization for Group B), the teacher initiated the intervention by asking the group to respond to the following: (a) "(Subject) seems to be having a problem. Who can tell (Subject) what the problem is?"; (b) "Can you tell (Subject) why that is a problem?"; (c) "Who can tell (Subject) what s/he needs to do to solve the problem?" If two students engaged in an inappropriate behavior simultaneously, the peer confrontation system was directed at both students (e.g., Johnny and Mary seem to be having a problem).

Following each question, the teacher selected a volunteer from the group to respond to that question. The teacher employed verbal praise to reinforce appropriate responses to the questions and to encourage the students' participation in the process. Additionally, the teacher used verbal praise to reinforce the student who had been confronted for accepting and engaging in the positive alternatives suggested by the group members. Intervention 1 conditions lasted 7 and 10 days for Group A and Group B, respectively.

> The teacher employed verbal praise to reinforce appropriate responses and to encourage student participation.

> Students said they preferred the peer confrontation system to the system used prior to the study.

Prior to instituting the peer confrontation system, the teacher received training in its implementation. The training focused on dealing with student responses, reinforcing appropriate behavior, and implementing the system in a positive, non-threatening manner. Before beginning the intervention, the teacher engaged in role-playing and practiced using the system with groups not included in the study. The training was conducted by the senior author of this article and lasted for 3 days.

Baseline 2

This period replicated the conditions described in Baseline 1. Baseline 2 conditions were maintained for 5 and 6 days for Group A and Group B, respectively.

Intervention 2

This phase was characterized by a return to the experimental conditions described in Intervention 1. Intervention 2 lasted 11 and 12 days for Group A and Group B, respectively.

RESULTS

The results are presented in Figures 1 and 2. The data indicate that the intervention led to a marked decrease in both groups' inappropriate behavior.

For Group A, the percentage of intervals of on-task behavior during Baseline 1 ranged from 29 to 62% with a mean of 44.1%. During Intervention 1 the percentage of intervals in which Group A exhibited on-task behavior increased to a mean of 84% with a range of 45 to 100%. The percentage of intervals of on-task behavior during Baseline 2 ranged from 43 to 64% with a mean of 57.4%. During Intervention 2 the percentage of intervals of on-task behavior yielded a mean of 87.5% with a range of 59 to 96%.

For Group B, the number of inappropriate verbalizations per minute during Baseline 1 ranged from .76 to 1.42 with a mean of 1.10. During Intervention 1 Group B's inappropriate verbalizations per minute decreased to a mean of .22 with a range of .06 to .52. The mean number of inappropriate verbalizations per minute during Baseline 2 was .52 with a range of .14 to .91. Data collected during Intervention 2 yielded a mean of .13 inappropriate verbalizations per minute with a range of 0 to .31.

Student Satisfaction Data

Students in both groups were interviewed individually by their teacher at the end of the study to determine their perceptions of the treatment conditions. Prior to the interview, the teacher assured the students that their comments would be used to help the teacher assist students in the class and would not be shared with anyone else. In the interview, students were asked to respond orally to the following:

1. Would you rather work the way we used to or under the peer confrontation system?
2. What did you like about the peer confrontation system?
3. What didn't you like about the peer confrontation system? and
4. Would you like to continue working using the peer confrontation system?

Of the 13 students, 11 said they preferred the peer confrontation system to the system used prior to the study. Students liked several things about the system including the problem-solving aspect and their ability to "work better and pay attention." The aspects of the system disliked by the students were "it was embarrassing (to be confronted)" and "sometimes it slowed the group." When asked if they would like to

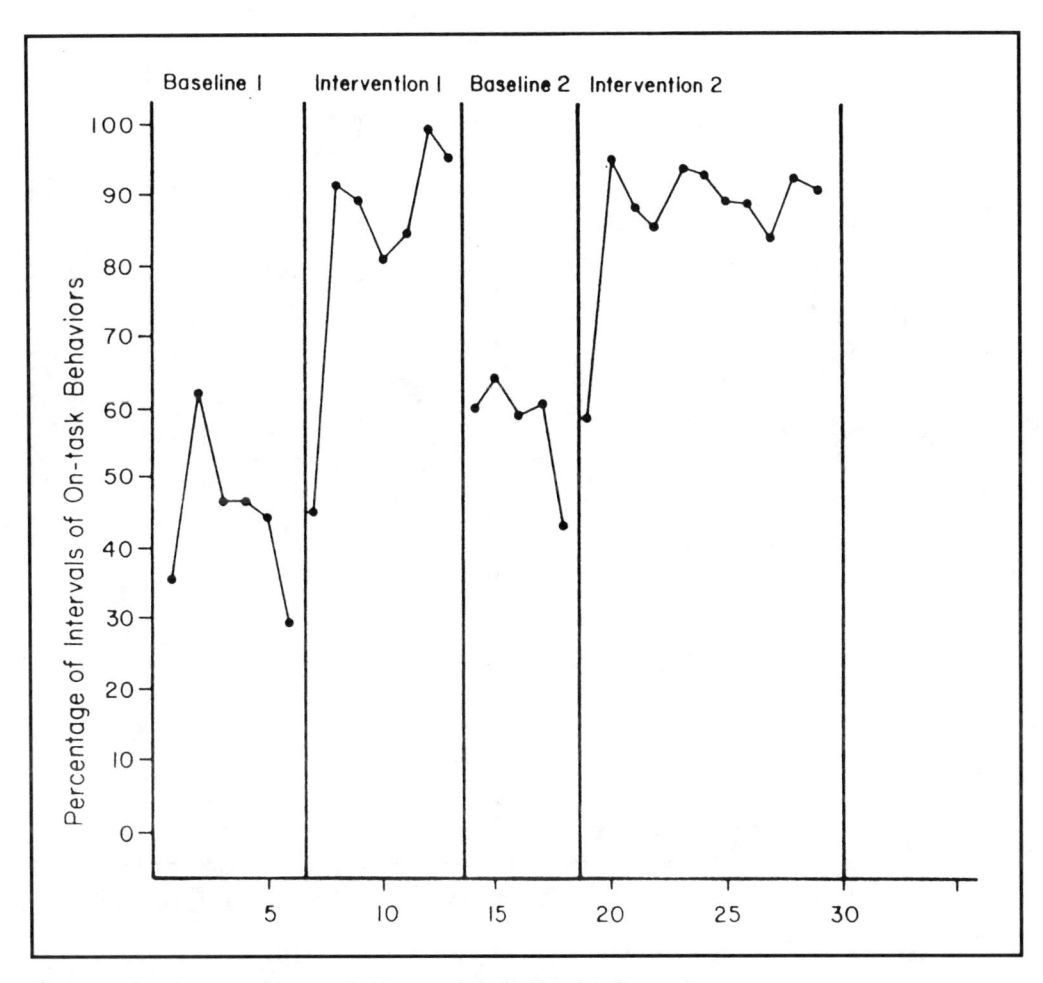

Figure 1. Percentage of intervals of on-task behavior for Group A.

continue the peer confrontation system, 12 of the 13 students responded in the affirmative.

DISCUSSION

The results of this study suggest that a peer confrontation system used in conjunction with a token economy system may be an effective method for decreasing inappropriate behavior of students in groups. This finding is consistent with and adds to the professional literature on peer confrontation (Bellafiore & Salend, 1983; Sandler et al., 1987). The teacher reported that when the intervention was in effect, she "was able to accomplish more and spent less time disciplining students." She also noted during the treatment sessions, "students completed more work and worked at a faster pace."

The system has several advantages. A unique aspect of the peer confrontation system is the problem-solving component. Through problem-solving, peers offer positive alternatives to the inappropriate behavior and become actively involved in the classes' behavior management system. For example, throughout this study peers told disruptive students to "not be distracted by other kids," "wait until the class is over before talking to someone," try to remember to raise your hand," and "concentrate

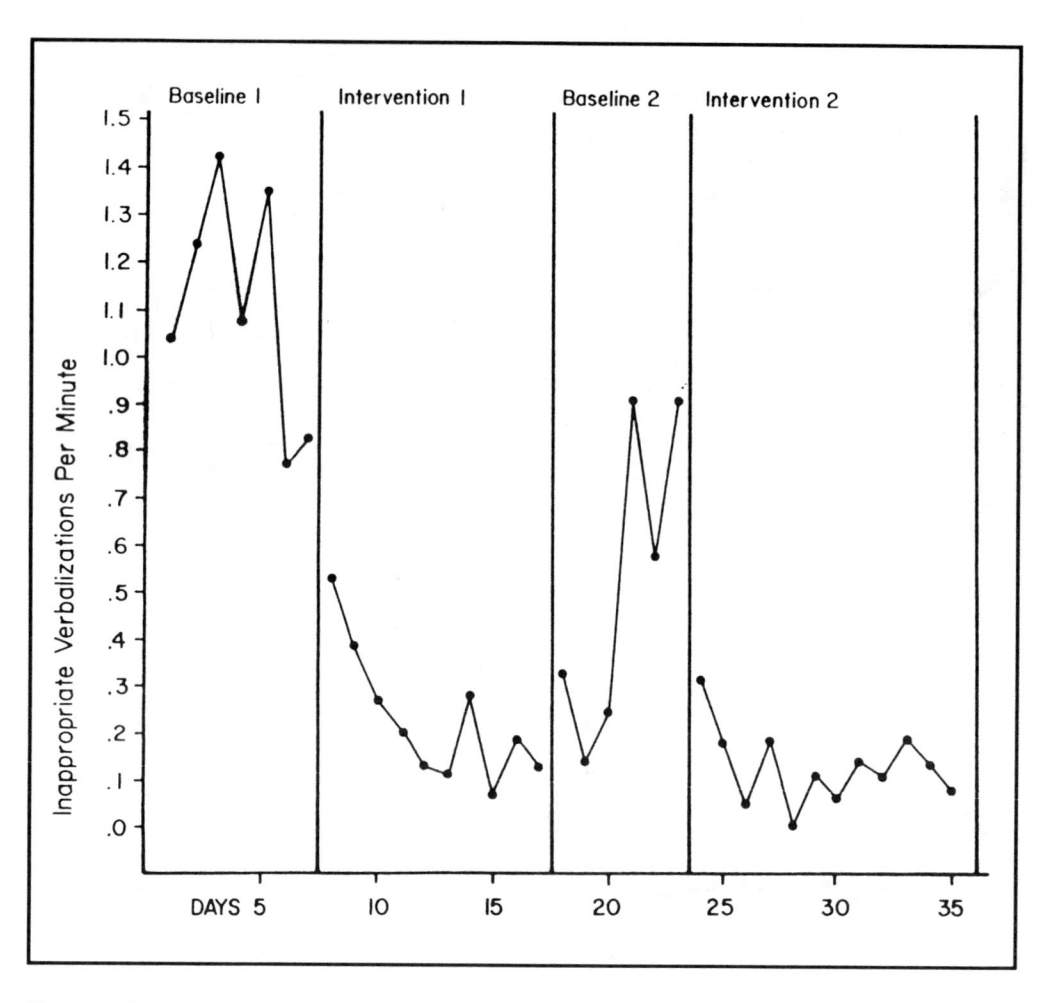

Figure 2. Inappropriate verbalizations per minute for Group B.

on listening to the teacher." Another advantage of the system is the students' positive reactions. Students were observed actively engaging in the process and occasionally initiated the procedure. Student satisfaction data indicated students liked the system and would like to continue using it. These findings are consistent with anecdotal reports that students enjoy the procedure and apply it spontaneously (Bellafiore & Salend, 1983; Sandler et al., 1987).

The system has several benefits for teachers. First, it is easy to implement and can be employed without taking a lot of teacher time or resources. Second, peer confrontation is a relatively natural consequence of misbehavior. Third, while containing elements of mild punishment, the intervention offers information to students about what to do and not merely what not to do. Finally, the system can be employed across a variety of behaviors and classroom settings.

The system also can be modified for implementation in mainstreamed settings. For example, to avoid the potential embarrassment that can be associated with directing the system toward the student who engaged in the inappropriate behavior (e.g., Dale seems to be having a problem. Who can tell Dale what the problem is?), the system can be adapted so that when any class member engages in the targeted inappropriate behavior, the class is viewed as having a problem (e.g., The class seems to be having a problem. Who can tell the class what the problem is?). Additionally, to minimize the teacher's involvement in the system, students can be taught to initiate and to manage the system.

Willems (1974) cautioned researchers to consider "the indirect and unintended effects of the intervention" (p. 161). He suggests that researchers examine the side effects of the intervention on behaviors, individuals, and settings as well as the timing of the effects. Because the peer confrontation system has elements of punishment and peer pressure (Bellafiore & Salend, 1983; Sandler et al., 1987), professionals should watch for the negative side effects associated with punishment (e.g., escape avoidance, withdrawn or aggressive behavior) and peer pressure based strategies (e.g., verbal threats, physically threatening gestures, aggressive acts; Alberto & Troutman, 1986; Axelrod, 1973).

In this study, while initially there was some grimacing and face hiding when the intervention was applied and one student felt it was embarrassing to be confronted, the potential risks of punishment and peer pressure were not evidenced. The potential deleterious effects of the use of aversives may not have been realized because the peer confrontation system provided instruction to students concerning what to do as well as what not to do. Additionally, the potential negative side effects of punishment and peer pressure may have been minimized because the intervention was applied to each member of the group rather than to a single targeted student. The fact that the teacher had previously established positive and accepting relationships with the students and was trained in the implementation of the system also served to lessen potential negative outcomes.

The results of this study should be interpreted with several reservations. While the teacher reported that student performance improved when the intervention was in effect, no data concerning work completion were collected. Future research should provide data to assess the impact of the intervention on measures of academic achievement. Because of time constraints associated with the end of the school year, the number of observations sessions were limited and data to determine the maintenance effects of the treatment were not provided. Subsequent studies should examine the efficacy of the treatment over a longer period of time and offer data to examine the maintenance of the treatment effects. While social validity data concerning the student's perceptions were collected, future studies also should address other social validity issues (e.g., selection of target behaviors). In light of the emphasis on educating students with disabilities in mainstreamed settings, research to examine the efficacy of a peer confrontation system in regular classroom settings is needed.

REFERENCES

Alberto, P. A., & Troutman, A. C. (1986). *Applied behavior analysis for teachers.* Columbus, OH: Merrill.

Axelrod, S. (1973). Comparison of individual and group contingencies in two special classes. *Behavior Therapy, 4,* 83-90.

Baer, D. M., Wolf, M. M., & Risley, T. R. (1968). Some current dimensions of applied behavior analysis. *Journal of Applied Behavior Analysis, 1,* 91-97.

Bellafiore, L. A., & Salend, S. J. (1983). Modifying inappropriate behavior through a peer confrontation system. *Behavioral Disorders, 8,* 274-279.

Candler, A., & Goodman, G. (1979). SPACE for students to manage behavior. *Academic Therapy, 15,* 87-90.

> Future research should (a) provide data to assess the impact of the intervention on measures of academic achievement and (b) examine the efficacy of a peer confrontation system in regular classroom settings.

Dedrick, S., & Lattyak, J. (1981). *Time concept series.* Beaverton, OR: Dormac.

Greenwood, C., & Hops, H. (1981). Group-oriented contingencies and peer behavior change. In P. Strain (Ed.), *Utilization of classroom peers as behavior change agents* (pp. 189-259). New York: Plenum.

Lemlech, J. K. (1979). *Classroom management.* New York: Harper & Row.

Nelson, C. M. (1981). Classroom management. In J. M. Kauffman & D. P. Hallahan (Eds.), *Handbook of special education* (pp. 663-687). Englewood Cliffs, NJ: Prentice-Hall.

Salend, S. J. (1983). Guidelines for explaining target behaviors to students. *Elementary School Guidance and Counseling, 18,* 88-93.

Salend, S. J. (1987). Group-oriented behavioral strategies. *Teaching Exceptional Children, 20,* 53-56.

Sandler, A. G., Arnold, L. B., Gable, R. A., & Strain, P. S. (1987). Effects of peer pressure on disruptive behavior of behaviorally disordered classmates. *Behavioral Disorders, 12,* 104-110.

Savicki, V. (1981). *Working with troubled children.* New York: Human Science.

Smith, L., & Fowler, S. (1984). Positive peer pressure: The effects of peer monitoring on children's disruptive behavior. *Journal of Applied Behavior Analysis, 17,* 213-227.

Solomon, R. W., & Wahler, R. G. (1973). Peer reinforcement control of classroom problem behavior. *Journal of Applied Behavior Analysis, 6,* 49-56.

Strain, P. S., & Odom, S. L. (1986). Peer social initiations: Effective interventions for social skill development of exceptional children. *Exceptional Children, 52,* 543-552.

Van Houten, R., Nau, P., Mackenzie-Keating, S., Sameoto, D., & Calavecchia, B. (1982). An analysis of some variables influencing the effectiveness of reprimands. *Journal of Applied Behavior Analysis, 15,* 65-83.

Vorrath, H., & Brendtro, L. (1974). *Positive peer culture.* Chicago: Aldine.

Wechsler, D. (1974). *Wechsler intelligence scale for children-revised.* San Antonio, TX: Psychological Corp.

Willems, E. P. (1974). Behavioral technology and behavioral ecology. *Journal of Applied Behavior Analysis, 7,* 151-165.

Woodruff, G. W., & Moore, G. N. (1984). *Working with words in spelling (Level B).* North Billerica, MA: Curriculum Associates.

Woodruff, G. W., & Moore, G. N. (1987). *Language skills (Level A).* North Billerica, MA: Curriculum Associates.

Social Interaction Training for Preschool Children with Behavioral Disorders

Mary A. McEvoy
Samuel L. Odom

ABSTRACT: The importance of early peer interaction for the development of positive outcomes on adult life adjustment measures has been well documented. Children who do not engage in social interaction, or do so at a depressed rate, do not have access to this avenue for skill development. The purpose of this article is to provide an illustrative review of the most recent advances in social interaction research for children who exhibit a wide range of behavioral disorders. Specifically, teacher-mediated, peer mediated, and interpersonal problem-solving approaches to promoting social interaction are presented. In addition, factors which affect social interaction training such as type of activities, presence of socially competent peers, and subject characteristics are discussed. Finally, suggestions for further research are advanced.

Reprinted from *Behavioral Disorders*, Vol. 12, Number 4, August 1987, pp. 242-251

Young children first begin to interact socially with their peers during infancy (Mueller & Vandell, 1979). These interactions grow in frequency and complexity and reach a plateau in the third and fourth years of life (Hartup, 1983). A convergence of research findings suggests that participation in social interactions with peers contributes directly to the acquisition of cognitive (Murray, 1972; Perret-Clermont, 1980; Piaget, 1926), social cognitive (Damon, 1984), language (Guralnick, 1981), and even more advanced social skills (Hartup & Sancilio, 1986). Children who do not engage in social interaction with peers, or who do so at a depressed rate, do not have access to this rich avenue for skill development. A number of researchers have documented the relationship between failure to establish positive peer relationships in childhood and negative outcomes on such adult life adjustment measures as referral for psychiatric treatment (Cowen, Peterson, Babigian, Izzo, & Trost, 1973), bad conduct discharges from the military (Roff, 1961), withdrawal from school prior to graduation (Ullmann, 1957), and juvenile delinquency (Roff, Sells, & Golden, 1972; West & Farrington, 1973).

Preparation of this article was supported by Grant No. G008630344 from the U. S. Department of Education, OSERS. The authors wish to thank Wilma Davis for her technical assistance.

> Researchers have developed and evaluated procedures for social interaction training for children with autism and socially withdrawn or isolate children.

In recent years a growing number of experimental studies have examined the problem of social skill development for preschool children with behavioral disorders. Specifically, researchers have developed and evaluated procedures for social interaction training for children with autism (Lord & Hopkins, 1986; McEvoy et al., 1987; McHale, 1983; Odom, Hoyson, Jamieson, & Strain, 1985; Odom & Strain, 1986) and socially withdrawn or isolate children (Furman, Rahe, & Hartup, 1979; Hecimovic, Fox, Shores, & Strain, 1985; Hendrickson, Strain, Tremblay, & Shores, 1982; Twardosz, Nordquist, Simon, & Botkin, 1983). Given the immediate and long-term significance of peer social interactions for preschool children with behavioral disorders and the documented delays that may occur in the development of their peer social interaction skills, an inclusion of social interaction skills as legitimate targets of instruction in preschool programs would seem appropriate. The purpose of this article is to provide an illustrative review of the most recent advances in social interaction research with preschool children who exhibit a range of behavioral disorders. Included within that group will be children who are socially withdrawn and children who are autistic. We will examine teacher-mediated, peer-mediated, and interpersonal problem-solving approaches to promoting social interaction skills. Factors affecting outcomes of social interaction training will be described and, finally, suggestions for future research will be advanced.

Teacher-Mediated Interventions

In a recent review of early intervention procedures for socially withdrawn preschool children, Mastropieri and Scruggs (1985) reported that teachers were major or minor intervenors in over 80% of the studies. The most typical form of teacher mediation is the use of prompting and positive reinforcement (e.g., praise) for appropriate social interaction. A number of studies have shown that teachers can increase the social interactions of preschool children with behavioral disorders (e.g., Allen, Hart, Buell, Harris, & Wolf, 1964; Hart, Reynolds, Baer, Brawley, & Harris, 1968; Strain, Shores, & Kerr, 1976; Strain & Timm, 1974; Strain & Weigerink, 1975; Timm, Strain, & Eller, 1979). More recently, Bryant and Budd (1984) evaluated the effectiveness of a teacher-mediated package for training behaviorally handicapped children to share. Teachers used a program developed by Barton and Ascione (1979) which consisted of instructions, modeling, behavioral rehearsal, and teacher prompts and praise for interaction. Substantial increases in sharing were seen for 5 of the 6 children who participated in the training. The authors also reported concomitant decreases in negative interactions.

Wolfe, Boyd, and Wolfe (1983) investigated the effects of verbal instructions and a token economy on the rate of cooperative play among preschool children with behavior problems. Three children who were aggressive or socially withdrawn were given "happy faces" and praised by the classroom teacher contingent upon cooperative play. In addition, children who received a predetermined number of "happy faces" were allowed 10 min of outdoor freeplay. Increases in cooperative play were seen for all 3 children when the intervention was implemented. The authors reported that the children maintained cooperative behavior after the intervention procedures were systematically faded, although the procedures were never eliminated completely.

While teacher-mediated procedures have effectively produced changes in the social interaction skills of preschoolers with behavioral disorders, researchers have identified several problems with this type of intervention. First, Strain, Cooke, and Apolloni (1976) reported that teacher-mediated procedures that incorporate a specific set of prompts and reinforcers have been evaluated primarily in highly structured training settings using well-trained practitioners. In addition, Strain and Fox (1981) reported that this technique may disrupt ongoing interactions. Odom and Strain (1986) compared teacher prompting procedures with a peer-mediated approach. In discussing the limitations of teacher-mediated procedures, they reported that the children with autism did not initiate interactions unless prompted by the teacher to do so. In addition, Timm, Strain, and Eller (1979) have pointed out the lengthy fading and learning process that is necessary when reducing teacher prompts. Clearly, more attention must be focused on designing teacher mediated procedures that can be implemented readily in the classroom setting and that do not require continuous use of teacher prompts and praise.

Recently, several researchers evaluated the use of teacher-mediated group affection activities to promote social interaction. Affection activities were developed by Twardosz et al. (1983) in response to some of the criticisms of teacher-mediated interventions discussed above. Those investigators were interested in designing procedures that would be relatively easy to implement by preschool teachers, would focus on functional social interaction behaviors, would provide opportunities for acquisition of new skills, could be implemented in the settings where increases in interaction were desired (thus addressing the generalization problem), and would involve multiple peers in training. In addition, Twardosz et al. (1983) were interested in the expression of affection and its relationship to other types of social interaction. Tremblay, Strain, Hendrickson, and Shores (1981) had found that physical affection was one of several social initiation categories that was likely to be responded to positively by peers. Twardosz et al. (1983) developed and evaluated procedures that would encourage the expression of affection and address the issues raised above.

A number of researchers (Brown, Ragland, & Fox, 1987; McEvoy et al., 1987; Twardosz et al., 1983) have now used group affection activities to increase the peer interactions of preschool children who were socially withdrawn or of autistic preschoolers. These activities occur during group time and are based upon typical preschool games, songs, and materials. At the start of the activity, the children greet each other by exchanging some form of physical affection such as a hug, pat on the back, high five, and so forth. The children then participate in an activity such as "farmer in the dell" or singing "If you're happy and you know it." However, these well-known preschool games and songs are modified to include an affection component. For example, instead of singing "the farmer takes a wife" or "the wife takes a child", the teacher might have the children "hug a wife" or "tickle a child." Not only has interaction been increased during the affection activities, but also during freeplay periods in which training did not occur. Twardosz et al. (1983) hypothesized that the procedures may be effective for several reasons: the pairing of peers with pleasurable experiences, desensitization to peer interaction, and/or teaching the handicapped children skills that facilitate freeplay interaction. Also, generalization may have been effected

> More attention must be focused on designing teacher mediated procedures that can be implemented readily in the classroom setting and that do not require continuous use of teacher prompts and praise.

> Peer-mediated interventions are based on the premise that children develop social skills through their interactions with peers.

by the use of multiple peers with more advanced social skills. The results from group affection studies activities are encouraging. However, given the limitations of the teacher-mediated procedures discussed above, many researchers have pursued the use of peer-mediated procedures as an alternative.

Peer-Mediated Intervention

Peer-mediated interventions are based on the premise that children develop social skills through their interactions with peers. An added assumption is that socially competent peers naturally interact with their young peers in ways that facilitate social skill acquisition and that they can be taught to use these interactions systematically to enhance the social skills of young children with behavioral disorders. Such interventions are called peer-mediated because the teacher does not directly prompt or reinforce the child with behavioral disorders in the intervention, but rather the intervention is delivered through the peer. Odom and Strain (1984a) identified three types of peer-mediated interventions. In *proximity interventions*, children with behavioral disorders are simply placed with socially competent peers and the effects due to this proximity are measured. For example, Furman et al. (1979) randomly assigned socially withdrawn preschool children to a small play group containing play partners of the same age, a small play group containing play partners 12 to 20 months younger, or in a no treatment control situation. Withdrawn children assigned to the cross-aged play group exhibited significantly higher levels of social interaction than did children in the other groups. Proximity interventions with elementary-aged children with autism have revealed similar increases in social interaction (Lord & Hopkins, 1986; McHale, 1983).

Prompt and reinforce strategies represent a second type of peer-mediated interventions. In these interventions, peers are taught to prompt the response that they want from a child with behavioral disorders, and then to provide reinforcement. For example, as part of his study in an integrated classroom, Nordquist (1978) taught preschoolers (a) to prompt an autistic classmate to imitate their motor behavior and then (b) to provide the autistic child with reinforcement after the behavior was imitated.

Peer-initiation strategies represent the most frequently used peer-mediated intervention for promoting social interaction skills (Strain & Odom, 1986). In this intervention, the teacher or investigator teaches socially competent peers to direct social initiations to the children with behavioral disorders. These peer intervenors are taught to persist in their social initiations because the behaviorally disordered peers may be unresponsive initially. When necessary, the teacher may provide verbal prompts to the peer intervenor or provide reinforcement to the intervenor at the end of the session if he or she reached an established criterion.

In an early peer-initiation study, Strain, Shores, and Timm (1977) taught a preschool peer to increase his social initiations to a socially withdrawn peer, and noted increases in the withdrawn child's social interaction. In a second study, Strain (1977) found generalized increases in socially withdrawn preschoolers' interactions with peers across settings when a peer intervenor began directing social initiations to the withdrawn child.

More recent research on peer-initiation interventions has examined the component features of the intervention package. To investigate the relative efficacy of the components of a peer-initiation intervention with 3 preschoolers with autism or other behavioral disorders, Odom et al. (1985) systematically analyzed the importance of reinforcement and teacher prompts for the *peer interventors* (i.e., children who delivered the treatment). They found that the peer intervenors continued to direct initiations to the target children when reinforcement was withdrawn, but their initiations decreased when teacher prompts were removed and increased when teacher prompts were reinstituted. The behaviorally disordered children's level of social interaction covaried with peers' limitations.

To reduce the peer intervenors' reliance on teacher verbal prompts, Odom and Watts (1987) used a correspondence training approach to teach the peer intervenor to continue initiating to the 3 autistic children in the absence of the teacher's verbal prompts. Peer intervenors were reinforced when they did what they said they were going to do. With this approach, peer intervenors' initiations continued when the teacher withdrew her prompts and the autistic children continued to interact. The number of peers included as intervenors in peer-initiation interventions is another variable that has been investigated. In teacher-mediated social interaction research with elementary-aged children and adolescents with autism, investigators have used multiple peer exemplars to promote peer and setting generalization of social interactions (Brady et al., 1984; Fox et al., 1984). To examine the use of multiple peer intervenors with preschool children, Odom, Strain, Karger, and Smith (1986) employed 3 peer intervenors in one peer-initiation intervention and compared its effects with a peer-initiation intervention with a single peer. Although total social interaction for the 2 target children, 1 autistic and 1 electively mute child, did not differ across interventions, the electively mute preschool child engaged in more frequent social initiations in both conditions during the latter phases of the study.

To compare the relative effects of a peer-initiation strategy with a teacher prompting intervention, Odom and Strain (1986) used an alternating treatments design with 3 autistic preschool children. During the teacher-mediated intervention, the teacher prompted the target child to interact with a peer and taught peers to respond and extend the interaction. During the peer-initiation intervention, peers were taught to direct social interactions to the target child, but not necessarily to respond. Autistic subjects' mean length of interaction was greater during the teacher prompting/peer response intervention, although the peer initiation intervention also produced substantial increases in the autistic children's social interaction. Although peer-mediated interventions appear to produce substantial changes in the social interactions of autistic and socially withdrawn preschoolers, researchers have presented little evidence for maintenance of these changes after the intervention is removed or clear evidence for cross-setting generalization. Both of these topics need to be examined in future research.

Interpersonal Social Problem-Solving Interventions

Interpersonal social problem-solving is a process by which children solve problems related to social interactions with peers. With preschool children from low sociometric status (SES) families, Spivak and Shure (1974) created an interpersonal problem-solving program containing 46 lessons that taught children both the linguistic prerequisites for problem-solving skills and how to

> Interpersonal social problem-solving is a process by which children solve problems related to social interactions with peers.

> Interpersonal social problem-solving appears to be a promising technique for children without disabilities, and tentative evidence exists for its effects upon the problem-solving skills of preschoolers who are withdrawn and aggressive.

generate alternative solutions to interpersonal problems. When implemented with low SES preschool children, these authors found substantial increases in the children's ability to generate alternative solutions to social problems in a test situation and also found positive changes on teacher ratings of social adjustment, which maintained at a one year follow-up.

Other researchers have examined the Spivak and Shure (1974) technique for training problem-solving skills. Sharp (1981) implemented an interpersonal problem-solving procedure with low SES children and found positive changes in preschoolers' verbal generation of problem-solving, but no changes in the children's behavior in the classroom. The absence of effect upon behavior in the classroom was replicated by Rickel, Eshelman, and Loigman (1983).

Extending Spivak and Shure's model, Ridley and Vaughn (1982) created a social problem-solving program composed of 53 lessons that emphasized language concepts, empathy, goal identification, generating alternative solutions, cue sensitivity, and goal identification. Relative to their control group, these authors found significant gains in social problem-solving as measured by a behavioral assessment in an analog situation, as well as increases in positive self-perception. In a replication of this study, Vaughn and Ridley (1983) observed increases in positive social interaction with peers in the classroom as a result of their intervention.

Social problem-solving researchers have most frequently conducted their research with preschool children who were normally developing, or who were at some risk for behavioral disorders through the socioeconomic status of their families. However, with a group of aggressive preschool children, Vaughn, Ridley, and Bullock (1984) implemented a social problem-solving intervention and found that children in their intervention group engaged in significantly more solutions to problems, measured by the Behavioral Interpersonal Problem-Solving Test (Ridley & Vaughn, 1982), than did children in a control group with direct adult contact. These differences maintained at a 6-month follow-up. With a group of preschool-aged children identified as emotionally disturbed (i.e., acting out or aggressive), Koenings and Oppenheimer (1985) trained role-taking skills using a small group format across 20 lessons. They found significant changes in the interventions group's ability to perceive emotional consequences and to take the perspective of others. However, neither of these studies tracked changes in classroom behavior.

In summary, interpersonal social problem-solving appears to be a promising technique for children without handicaps, and tentative evidence exists for its effects upon the problem-solving skills of withdrawn and aggressive preschoolers. Future research should examine the effects of these interventions upon the classroom behavior with children with behavioral disorders.

Contextual Factors Affecting the Success of Interventions

Social interaction interventions for behaviorally disordered preschool children exist in a rich environmental context. Within this context, a range of factors may affect the ultimate outcomes of interventions (Strain & Kohler, in press). Although a full review is beyond the scope of this article, two factors that appear to have particularly powerful effects on social interaction intervention are the classroom activities in which the children with behavioral disorders participate and the characteristics of the peers with whom the children may interact.

Activities. The type of activity in which children engage their peers determines to a large degree whether children will interact with other children or engage in solitary play. Although few studies have been conducted with behaviorally disordered children, studies with preschool children who exhibit other handicaps may be instructive. Stoneman, Cantrell, and Hoover-Dempsey (1983) observed the types of activities around which preschool handicapped children in mainstreamed classes interacted. Cooperative play occurred most frequently around block activities, vehicles, and water play. Solitary play occurred most often around library, fine motor, and art activities.

In another observational study occurring in an integrated setting, DeKlyen and Odom (1987) classified a large number of play activities according to the degree of structure that each contained. Structure was defined as the amount of definition inherent in the activity (i.e., well-specified roles, clear behavioral requirements) as well as the amount of definition that the teacher initially provided. Frequency of social interaction was significantly related to the degree of structure in the activities. Interestingly, negative correlations existed for the level of teacher interactions in most activities and the level of social interaction with peers, thus supporting the findings of an earlier study by Shores, Hester, and Strain (1976).

To explain the variability during the treatment phase of an intervention study with behaviorally disordered children, Odom and Strain (1984b) examined the relative effectiveness of the intervention in different activities. They found that the intervention was much more effective in certain types of activities (e.g., sociodramatic play) than in other types of interventions (e.g., fine motor activities). In sum, activities which are made available and/or the activities which children elect to engage affect the level of social interaction, thus modifying the effectiveness of social interaction interventions.

Presence of socially competent peers. One can train children with behavioral disorders to interact with their peers, but unless there are socially responsive peers with whom to interact, it would not seem reasonable to expect social interactions to continue in the absence of intervention or to generalize to other classroom settings. Strain (1983) examined the cross-setting generalization of a peer-mediated intervention with autistic preschool children, and found that the autistic children did generalize treatment gains to a setting containing normally developing peers, but not to one containing only handicapped peers. In a second study, Strain (1984) found that cross-setting generalization also occurred only when the peer group had been coached to respond to the interaction of the autistic child. However, Hecimovic et al. (1985) were unable to replicate this finding with a second group of preschool children with behavioral disorders. Similarly, in the Odom et al. (1985) examination of cross-setting generalization of the effects of a peer-mediated intervention, the presence of normally developing peers did not facilitate cross-setting generalization. From these it appears that the presence of socially responsive peers is a desirable condition for promoting social interaction, but not a sufficient condition. Further research must address the factors in addition to the presence of normally developing peers that mediate generalization.

> One can train children with behavioral disorders to interact with their peers, but unless there are socially responsive peers with whom to interact, it would not seem reasonable to expect social interactions to continue in the absence of intervention or to generalize to other classroom settings.

> Literature has established that interventions can be implemented successfully to increase the positive social interaction of children with behavioral disorders.

Subject Characteristics

As noted above, the broad classification of behavioral disorders includes children with a wide range of characteristics. It seems reasonable that children who are socially withdrawn might respond differently to certain social interaction interventions than would children who are aggressive or autistic. The characteristics of the child will play a major role in determining the success of the intervention, and should be considered closely when a teacher selects an intervention strategy to use with a child.

Several of the interventions described above (e.g., Spivak and Shure, 1974) require that the child have some verbal skills (i.e., social problem-solving, social coaching). Although there is some evidence that aggressive and socially withdrawn children may benefit from those interventions (Vaughn & Ridley, 1983), it seems highly likely that autistic children, because of their limited language skills, would not benefit. Socially withdrawn and autistic preschoolers appear to benefit from peer-mediated interventions, yet it is unlikely that such interventions would be as effective with aggressive children or ethically amenable for peer intervenors (i.e., the peer initiations could elicit aggressive behaviors toward the peer intervenor). In addition, group affection training activities appear more effective with socially withdrawn preschool children than with autistic children (McEvoy et al., 1987). For an intervention to be successful, an appropriate match must occur between the prerequisite skill requirements of the intervention and the characteristics of the preschool child with behavioral disorders.

Conclusions and Future Directions for Research

Over the past decade a growing body of literature has established that interventions can be implemented successfully to increase the positive social interaction of children with behavioral disorders. Earlier studies tested the effects of adult social reinforcement on social behavior (Allen et al., 1964; Buell, Stoddard, Harris, & Baer, 1968; Hart et al., 1968). Recently, researchers have begun to investigate the use of teacher-mediated group affection procedures to increase the rate of social interaction (Brown et al., 1987; McEvoy et al., 1987; Twardosz et al., 1983). However, due to the powerful influence peers have on children's behavior, much of the recent research has employed a peer-mediated approach (e.g., Odom et al., 1985; Odom et al., 1986; Odom & Watts, 1987). In addition, for young children with verbal skills, social problem-solving interventions have proven effective in increasing social interaction.

While researchers have been successful in increasing the social interaction skills of children with behavioral disorders, the current research has several limitations. First, the issue of generalization and maintenance must be addressed in future research. Appropriate social interaction skills must occur in situations outside of the training setting and they must maintain across time. While researchers have produced impressive treatment effects, there has been an inconsistent demonstration of cross-setting generalization and maintenance (Odom & Strain, 1984a). Stokes and Osnes (1987) have pointed out a number of procedures that could be included in training programs to promote generalization and maintenance. These include taking advantage of natural communities of reinforcement, training diversely, and incorporating functional mediators (e.g., use of common physical and social stimuli). Future research should be sensitive to the need to develop procedures that are easily implemented by classroom teachers and actively program for generalization and maintenance. In addition, much of the research to date has investigated procedures to increase the frequency of certain categories of interaction (e.g., initiations and response). Whether simple increases in the quantity of these behaviors is appropriate is an empirical question. For example, data from the Hendrickson et al. (1982) study suggested that after a certain point, increases in handicapped children's rate of initiations did not necessarily increase rate of responses to those initiations. The suggestion that "more is better" is an area that deserves future empirical analysis.

A second limitation of the current research is the use of global quantitative measures of social interaction as opposed to qualitative measures. In the recent past, researchers have assessed global measures of social interaction (e.g., positive social interaction, initiations, responses; Allen et al., 1964; Strain & Timm, 1974). When researchers have developed behavioral taxonomies that are more descriptive than the often-used global measures of social interactions, the single criterion for selection of behaviors was the probability that the behavior would elicit a positive social response from a peer (Nordquist, Twardosz, McEvoy, & Wilson, 1981; Strain, Odom, & McConnell, 1984; Tremblay et al., 1981).

A broader view of children's social interaction is needed. When children interact with their peers, they have a purpose which they intend to achieve (i.e., an *intended* function). They may use different behaviors to achieve the function, and these behaviors will have differential probabilities of success (i.e., actually achieving the function). Children with behavioral problems may encounter difficulties in peer interactions either because they do not choose the correct functions to pursue in a given context, they use less successful behaviors to achieve the desired functions, or they simply do not engage in any functional interactions. Odom, McEvoy, Ostrosky, and Bishop (1987) are currently field testing an observational procedure for measuring the functional characteristics of children's social interactions and specific behaviors that make up those interactions. Future research in this area could have relevance for the selection of target behaviors in interventions for children with behavioral disorders.

Finally, Strain and Kohller (in press) have called on researchers to assess the social validity of their intervention procedures. They urge that attention be given to the social acceptability of the procedures, the social significance of the target behaviors, and the social importance of the behavior change to the consumers; that is, do increases in social interactions achieve the ultimate goal of increases in friendships or social support relationships between individuals? Future research is needed on the development and evaluation of procedures that address these broader outcome variables.

REFERENCES

Allen, K. E., Hart, B., Buell, J. S., Harris, F. R., & Wolf, M. M. (1964). Effects of social reinforcement on isolate behavior of a nursery school child. *Child Development, 35,* 511-518.

Barton, E. J., & Ascione, F. R. (1979). Sharing in preschool children: Facilitation, stimulus generalization, response generalization, and maintenance. *Journal of Applied Behavior Analysis, 12,* 417-430.

Brady, M. P., Shores, R. E., Gunter, P., McEvoy, M. A., Fox, J. J., & White, C. (1984). Generalization of a severely handicapped adolescent's social interaction responses via multiple peers in a classroom setting. *Journal*

> When children interact with their peers, they have a purpose which they intend to achieve.

of the Association for Persons with Severe Handicaps, 9, 278-286.

Brown, W. H., Ragland, E. V., & Fox, J. J. (1987). *Effects of group socialization procedures on the social interactions of preschool children.* Manuscript submitted for publication.

Bryant, L. E., & Budd, K. S. (1984). Teaching behaviorally handicapped preschool children to share. *Journal of Applied Behavior Analysis,* 17(1), 45-56.

Buell, J. S., Stoddard, T., Harris, F. R., & Baer, D. M. (1968). Collateral social development accompanying reinforcement of outdoor play in a preschool child. *Journal of Applied Behavior Analysis, 1,* 167-173.

Cowen, E. L., Peterson, A., Babigian, H., Izzo, L. D., & Trost, M. A. (1973). Long term follow-up of early detected vulnerable children. *Journal of Consulting and Clinical Psychology, 41,* 438-446.

Damon, W. (1984). Peer education: The untapped potential. *Journal of Applied Developmental Psychology, 5,* 331-334.

DeKlyen, M., & Odom, S. L. (1987). *Structure and preschool peer interactions: Beyond the mainstream.* Manuscript submitted for publication.

Fox, J. J., Gunter, P., Brady, M. P., Bambara, L. M., Speigel-McGill, P., & Shores, R. E. (1984). Using multiple peer exemplars to develop generalized social responding of an autistic girl. In R. B. Rutherford, Jr. & C. Michael Nelson (Eds.), *Severe Behavior Disorders of Children and Youth* (Vol. 7, pp. 17-26). Reston, VA: Council for Children with Behavioral Disorders.

Furman, W., Rahe, D., & Hartup, W. (1979). Rehabilitation of socially withdrawn preschool children through mixed-age and same-age socialization. *Child Development,* 50(4), 915-922.

Guralnick, M. J. (1981). Peer influences on development of communicative competence. In P. Strain (Ed,), *The utilization of peers as behavior change agents* (pp. 31-68). New York: Plenum.

Hart, B. M., Reynolds, N. J., Baer, D. M., Brawley, E. R., & Harris, F. R. (1968). Effect of contingent and noncontingent social reinforcement on the cooperative play of a preschool child. *Journal of Applied Behavior Analysis, 1,* 73-76.

Hartup, W. W. (1983). Peer relations. In M. Heatherington (Ed.), *Handbook of Child Psychology* (Vol. 4, pp. 103-196). New York: John Wiley & Sons.

Hartup, W. W., & Sancilio, M. F. (1986). Children's friendships. In E. Schopler & G. Mesibov (Eds.), *Social behavior in autism* (pp. 61-80). New York: Plenum.

Hecimovic, A., Fox, J. J., Shores, R. E., & Strain, P. S. (1985). An analysis of developmentally integrated and segregated freeplay setting and the generalization of newly-acquired social behaviors of socially withdrawn preschoolers. *Behavioral Assessment, 7,* 367-388.

Hendrickson, J. M., Strain, P. S., Tremblay, A., & Shores, R. E. (1982). Interactions of behaviorally handicapped preschoolers: Functional effects of peer social initiations. *Behavior Modification, 6,* 323-353.

Koenings, A., & Oppenheimer, L. (1985). Development and training of role-taking abilities with emotionally disturbed preschoolers: A pilot study. *Journal of Applied Developmental Psychology, 6,* 313-320.

Lord, C., & Hopkins, J. M. (1986). The social behavior of autistic children with younger and same-aged nonhandicapped peers. *Journal of Autism and Developmental Disorders, 16,* 249-262.

Mastropieri, M. A., & Scruggs, T. E. (1985). Early intervention for socially withdrawn children. *Journal of Special Education,* 19(4), 427-441.

McEvoy, M. A., Nordquist, V. M., Twardosz, S., Heckaman, K. A., Wehby, J. H., & Denny, R. K. (1987). *Promoting autistic children's peer interaction in integrated early childhood settings using affection activities and incidental teaching.* Manuscript submitted for publication.

McHale, S. (1983). Social intervention of autistic and nonhandicapped children during freeplay. *American Journal of Orthopsychiatry,* 53(1), 81-91.

Mueller, E., & Vandell, D. (1979). Infant-infant interaction. In J. Osofsky (Ed.). *Handbook of infant development* (pp. 714-756). New York: John Wiley & Sons.

Murray, F. (1972). The acquisition of conservation through social interaction. *Developmental Psychology, 6,* 1-6.

Nordquist, V. M. (1978). A behavioral approach to the analysis of peer interactions. In M. Guralnick (Ed.), *Early intervention and the integration of handicapped and nonhandicapped children* (pp. 53-84). Baltimore: University Park Press.

Nordquist, V. M., Twardosz, S., McEvoy, M. A., & Wilson, S. (1981*). Project SEARCH: Observer training manual.* Unpublished manuscript, University of Tennessee, Knoxville.

Odom, S. L., Hoyson, M., Jamieson, B., & Strain, P. S. (1985). Increasing handicapped preschoolers peer social interactions: Cross setting and component analysis. *Journal of Applied Behavior Analysis, 18,* 3-16.

Odom, S. L., McEvoy, M. A., Ostrosky, M., & Bishop, L. (1987, May). *Measuring the functional social interaction of preschool children.* Paper presented at the meeting of the Association of Behavior Analysis, Nashville, TN.

Odom, S. L,, & Strain, P. S. (1984a). Peer-mediated approaches to increasing children's social interactions: A review. *American Journal of Orthopsychiatry, 54,* 544-557.

Odom, S. L., & Strain, P. S. (1984b). Classroom-based social skills instruction for severely handicapped preschool children. *Topics in Early Childhood Special Education, 4,* 97-116.

Odom, S. L., & Strain, P. S. (1986). A comparison of peer-initiation and teacher-antecedent interventions for promoting reciprocal social interaction of autistic preschoolers. *Journal of Applied Behavior Analysis, 19*(1), 59-71.

Odom, S. L., Strain, P. S., Karger, M. A., & Smith, J. D. (1986). Using single and multiple peers to promote social interaction of preschool children with handicaps. *Journal of the Division of Early Childhood, 10,* 53-64.

Odom, S. L., & Watts, E. (1987). *Cross setting generalization of autistic preschool children's social interaction in peer-initiation intervention.* Manuscript to be submitted for publication.

Perret-Clermont, A. N. (1980). Social interaction and cognitive development in children. *European Monographs in Social Psychology.* London: Academic Press.

Piaget, J. (1926). *The language and thought of the child.* London: Routledge & Kegen Paul.

Rickel, A. V., Eshelman, A. K., & Loigman, G. A. (1983). Social problem-solving training: A follow-up study of cognitive and behavioral effects. *Journal of Abnormal Child Psychology, 11,* 15-28.

Ridley, C. A., & Vaughn, S. R. (1982). The effects of a preschool problem-solving program on interpersonal behavior. *Journal of Applied Developmental Psychology, 3,* 177-180.

Roff, M. (1961). Childhood social interactions and young adult bad conduct. *Journal of Abnormal Social Psychology, 63,* 333-337.

Roff, M., Sells, B., & Golden, M. M. (1972). *SST2 Social adjustment and personality in children.* Minneapolis: University of Minnesota Press.

Sharp, K. C. (1981). Impact of interpersonal problem-solving training on preschoolers' social competency. *Journal of Applied Developmental Psychology, 2,* 129-143.

Shores, R. E., Hester, P., & Strain, P. S. (1976). The effects of amount and type of teacher-child interaction on child-child interaction during freeplay. *Psychology in the Schools, 13,* 171-175.

Spivak, G., & Shure, M. B. (1974). *Social adjustment of young children: A cognitive approach to solving real-life problems.* San Francisco: Jossey-Bass.

Stokes, T. F., & Osnes, P. G. (1987). Programming generalization of children's social behavior. In P. Strain, M. Guralnick, & H. Walker (Eds.), *Children's social behavior: Development, assessment, and intervention* (pp. 408-443). New York: Academic Press.

Stoneman, Z.. Cantrell, M. L., & Hoover-Dempsey, K. (1983). The association between play materials and social behavior in a mainstreamed preschool: A naturalistic investigation. *Journal of Applied Developmental Psychology, 4,* 163-174.

Strain, P. S. (1977). An experimental analysis of peer social initiations on the behavior of withdrawn preschool children: Some training and generalization effects. *Journal of Abnormal Psychology, 5,* 445-455.

Strain, P. S. (1983). Generalization of autistic children's social behavior change: Effects of developmentally integrated and segregated settings. *Analysis and Intervention in Developmental Disabilities, 3,* 23-34.

Strain, P. S. (1984). Social interaction of handicapped preschoolers in developmentally integrated and segregated settings: A study of generalization effects. In T. Field (Ed.), *Friendship between normally developing and handicapped children* (pp. 187-208). Chicago: Society for Research in Child Development.

Strain, P. S., Cooke, T. P., & Apolloni, T. A. (1976). *Teaching exceptional children: Assessing and modifying social behavior.* New York: Academic Press.

Strain, P. S., & Fox, J. J. (1981). Peer social initiations and the modification of social withdrawal: A review and future perspective. *Journal of Pediatric Psychology, 6,* 417-433.

Strain, P. S., & Kohler, F. W. (in press). Social skill intervention with young handicapped children. In S. Odom & M. Karnes (Eds.), *Research in early childhood special education.* Paul Brookes Publishing.

Strain, P. S., & Odom, S. L. (1986). Peer social initiations: Effective intervention for social skill development of exceptional children. *Exceptional Children, 52,* 543-552.

Strain, P. S., Odom, S. L., & McConnell, S. R. (1984). Promoting social reciprocity of exceptional children: Identification, target behavior selection, and intervention. *Remedial and Special Education, 5,* 526-531.

Strain, P. S., Shores, R. E., & Kerr, M. M. (1976). An experimental analysis of "spillover" effects on the social interaction of behaviorally handicapped preschool children, *Journal of Applied Behavior Analysis, 9,* 31-40.

Strain. P. S., Shores, R. E., & Timm, M. (1977). Effects of peer social initiations on the behavior of withdrawn preschool children. *Journal of Applied Behavior Analysis, 10,* 289-298.

Strain, P. S. & Timm, M. (1974). An experimental analysis of social interaction between a behaviorally disordered preschool child and her classroom peers. *Journal of Applied Behavior Analysis, 7(4),* 583-590.

Strain, P. S., & Weigerink, R. (1976). The effects of sociodramatic activities on social interaction among behaviorally disordered preschool children. *Journal of Special Education, 10,* 71-75.

Timm, M., Strain, P. S., & Eller, P. (1979). Effects of systematic response dependent fading and thinning procedures on the maintenance of child-child interaction. *Journal of Applied Behavior Analysis,* 12(2), 308.

Tremblay, A., Strain, P. S., Hendrickson, J. M., & Shores, R. E. (1981). Social interactions of normal preschool children. *Behavior Modification, 5,* 237-253.

Twardosz, S., Nordquist, V. M., Simon, R., & Botkin, D. (1983). The effect of group affection activities on the interaction of socially isolate children. *Analysis and Intervention in Developmental Disabilities, 13,* 311-338.

Ullman, C. A. (1957). Teachers, peers, and tests as predictors of adjustment. *Journal of Educational Psychology, 48,* 257-267.

Vaughn, S. R., & Ridley, C. A. (1983). A preschool interpersonal problem-solving program: Does it affect behavior in the classroom? *Child Study Journal, 13,* 1-12.

Vaughn, S. R., Ridley, C. A., & Bullock, D. D. (1984). Interpersonal problem-solving skills training with aggressive young children. *Journal of Applied Developmental Psychology, 5,* 213-223

West, D. J., & Farrington, D. P. (1973). *Who becomes delinquent?* London: Heineman Press.

Wolfe, V. V., Boyd, L. A., & Wolfe, D. A. (1983). Teaching cooperative play to behavior problem preschool children. *Education and Treatment of Children,* 6(l), 1-9.

Entrapment Effects and the Generalization and Maintenance of Social Skills Training for Elementary School Students with Behavioral Disorders

Scott R. McConnell

Effective social interaction is a desired goal for all children. Social interaction provides opportunities for learning and practice of language, motor, and other skills (Hartup, 1983; Hops, Finch, & McConnell, 1985), and provides children with opportunities to play and work with others. Further, skills for social interaction are associated with and thought necessary for adjustment and achievement in schools (Green, Vosk, Forehand, Beck, & Vosk, 1980; McConnell et al., 1984), families (Patterson, 1982), and work settings (Warrenfeltz et al., 1981).

Because of these relationships, attention to social interaction skills is especially important for children with behavioral disorders. By definition, these children experience difficulties interacting with others (Kauffman, 1985). Such interactive difficulties lead to rejection by peers, social isolation, and reduced access to opportunities to benefit from social interaction with nonhandicapped peers (Strain, Odom, & McConnell, 1984; Walker, McConnell, & Clarke, 1985). Together, characteristics that lead to initial identification of behavioral disorders, as well as the primary treatment of these disorders in restricted educational settings, put identified children at risk for continued and future difficulties interacting with peers.

For these reasons, and a host of others (Hops et al., 1985), social skills training has recently become a major focus of research and treatment efforts for young children with behavioral disorders. This surge of interest and concern has led to a proliferation of *assessment* procedures for identifying social skills deficits among children, and *treatment* procedures for remediating these identified deficits.

These assessment and treatment procedures have been reviewed extensively, both in this journal (Schloss, Schloss, Wood, & Kiehl, 1986) and other sources (e.g., Cartledge & Milburn, 1980; Gresham, 1986; Hops et al., 1985; Hops & Greenwood, 1981, in press; Van Hasselt, Hersen, Whitehall, & Bellack, 1979). Typically, these reviews have focused on specific child characteristics and their implications for assessment and

Reprinted from *Behavioral Disorders, Vol. 12, Number 4,* August 1987, pp. 252-263

> Entrapment is a behavioral process by which newly acquired social responses come under the control of naturally occurring reinforcers.

treatment; relatively less attention has been paid to *interaction* variables that influence the development of social competence by handicapped and high-risk youngsters.

Attention to interaction variables may be one way of increasing our understanding of generalization and maintenance effects in social interaction skills training. Behavioral researchers, including those interested in social skills, have increased their efforts to identify procedures that will enhance generalization and maintenance of treatment (Stokes & Baer, 1977; Stokes & Osnes, 1986). In their recent review, Stokes and Osnes identify one class of generalization enhancement strategies as those that "take advantage of natural communities of reinforcement" (p. 418). Within this class of strategies, these authors place particular emphasis on the importance of social interactive relationships that will produce durable changes in target behaviors.

Rather than review assessment and treatment issues generally, the purpose of this article is to discuss recent research trends that focus on interaction variables that contribute to generalization and maintenance in social skills interventions for behaviorally disordered elementary school children. In particular, this article will outline one interactive phenomenon—entrapment—and argue that this conceptualization of social behavior offers special promise for developing and evaluating social skill interventions. Based on this discussion, the author will review several factors to be considered in selection of target behaviors for intervention. Finally, recently developed treatment packages (and adaptations of existing packages) that appear to target those variables related to the entrapment of adaptive social behavior by behaviorally handicapped elementary school students will be examined.

Entrapment: A Conceptual Framework for Social Interaction Skills Training

Entrapment is a behavioral process by which newly acquired social responses come under the control of naturally occurring reinforcers; these reinforcers are, by and large, the social behaviors of peers. [The author notes the potentially negative connotation of the term *entrapment* that is used here to identify a generally desirable phenomenon. However, it has been elected to use the term to preserve continuity with earlier work in this area (cf., Baer & Wolf, 1970; Kohler & Greenwood, 1986).] Entrapment describes one mechanism by which all children may develop and elaborate those behaviors termed *social skills*. For example, early in the school experience a child may offer a toy to a peer. This *share offer* is very likely to set the occasion for a positive peer response (Tremblay, Strain, Hendrickson, & Shores, 1981) and to be reciprocated by peers offering toys to the child in the future (cf., Charlesworth & Hartup, 1967; Kohler & Fowler, 1985). If positive interaction and reciprocated sharing serve as reinforcers for the child, sharing is likely to become entrapped: The likelihood of future share offers by the child is thus increased by exposure to naturally occurring social behaviors of others.

Social interaction is bidirectional and reciprocal (Strain & Shores, 1977), requiring the interrelated behavior of two or more individuals to occur. Hops and Greenwood (in press) compare social interaction to a tennis match; each interaction begins when one person's "serve" (or social initiation) is followed by another's "return" (or social response). After the initial exchange, interactions continue as a series of "volleys" with each person's behavior serving as both response and antecedent to the social behavior of the other. In this way, interaction unfolds with its overall content mutually determined by the ongoing, interdependent behavior of the interactants.

It is in this reciprocal, bidirectional process that newly acquired behaviors come into contact with naturally occurring reinforcing responses and that entrapment occurs. Entrapment may thus represent an essential feature of social skill interventions for behaviorally disordered children. To guarantee generalized and durable behavior change, we must teach children to exhibit those behaviors that will be naturally reinforced by peers. Further, at times we must restructure existing reinforcement contingencies in peer play groups, such that these new contingencies will maintain newly acquired adaptive social behaviors exhibited by children receiving our training.

Simply put, this conceptualization of entrapment as a primary process in the acquisition, maintenance, and generalization of social behaviors leads to an increased emphasis on interaction variables in social skills assessment and treatment for behaviorally disordered children. Attention to entrapment expands our assessment focus to include not only the social behavior of an individual child, but also the behavior of others in the child's environment; in particular, assessment must describe peer or teacher behavior that serves to reinforce and maintain adaptive or maladaptive social responding by the target child. Similarly, emphasis on the process of entrapment leads to changes in intervention procedures including (a) increased attention to training and coaching that teaches identified children to produce critical social interaction skills, and (b) more direct focus on peer behaviors that are likely to contribute to mutually dependent "entrapped" relationships that will maintain target behaviors long after intervention is ended. Thus, attention to interactive variables in social skills training may enhance the identification of *essential target behaviors* and the development of *effective treatment procedures* that lead to entrapment of adaptive social responses for children with behavioral disorders. We now turn to these two issues.

Selecting Target Behaviors for Social Interaction Skills Training

This analysis of entrapment would suggest that careful selection of target behaviors is critical to success in social skills training for children with behavioral disorders. In particular, intervention programs should include training for those skills and behaviors that (a) are adaptive or desirable and contribute to development of social competence for the handicapped child, and (b) prompt peer responses that are likely to serve as reinforcers, thus ontributing to the entrapment of the targeted behavior.

To guarantee these outcomes, skills included in any training program should be selected empirically, based on these two criteria (Hops et al., 1985). To date, however, this empirical basis has not been considered routinely in target behavior selection for social skill interventions. Rather, skills are often drawn from logical analyses of social interaction or peer acceptance, or from extrapolations of empirical work completed with adults. Both practices have been criticized (Foster & Ritchey, 1979; Hops & Greenwood, 1981; Strain et al., 1984).

Recently, however, several reviewers in this area have offered conceptual

---

Attention to interactive variables in social skills training may enhance the identification of *essential target behaviors* and the development of *effective treatment procedures* that lead to entrapment of adaptive social responses for children with behavioral disorders.

> The history of social skills training with children with behavioral disorders is replete with studies in which children demonstrate significant gains during treatment but fail to maintain these gains after intervention ends.

guidelines for the empirical selection of social skills. In one of the most complete works on entrapment of social behavior in children available to date, Kohler and Greenwood (1986) describe five necessary forms of evidence for the identification of behavioral entrapment; three of these rules have direct bearing on the selection of target behaviors for social skills interventions. To maximize the likelihood of entrapment for social skills included in our interventions, we must:

1. *Select behaviors that will be maintained after intervention is terminated.* Social skills training is typically designed to increase (or in some cases decrease) specific social behaviors to criterion or therapeutic levels of occurrence. To guarantee effectiveness and efficiency of these interventions, target skills must be selected that are most likely to be maintained at higher or more desired rates of occurrence by exposure to naturally occurring reinforcers after the period of intervention ends.

This point may seem obvious and not worth mentioning. However, the history of social skills training with behaviorally disordered children is replete with studies in which children demonstrate significant gains during treatment, but fail to maintain these gains after intervention ends (Hops, 1982). For example, Bornstein, Bellack, and Hersen (1980) trained four aggressive children between the ages of 8 and 12 to improve three specific aspects of positive assertiveness: increased eye contact, decreased use of hostile voice tone, and increased requests for new behavior. Although improvement was noted during treatment for all subjects across all three target behaviors, only one of the individually targeted behaviors (reduced use of hostile tone) continued at a similar level 4 to 26 weeks after training ended; for two subjects, decreasing trends were noted in requests for new behavior, and one child declined to pretreatment levels on the measure of eye contact. Thus, children maintained only one of three target behaviors, reduced use of hostile voice tone.

Given these findings, we can hypothesize that only reduced use of hostile voice tone came under the control of naturally occurring reinforcement from peers. It should be noted that multiple reasons may exist for maintenance and generalization of social skills, and that data presented by Bornstein and his colleagues (1980) is but one piece of a more comprehensive proof for the existence of behavioral entrapment (Kohler & Greenwood, 1986). However, to guarantee the efficiency and overall effectiveness of social skills training, particular attention must be given to identifying those skills that are most likely to be maintained long after training is completed.

2. *Select skills that will generalize a cross settings or other behaviors. Social skills training* typically occurs in one particular setting (e.g., a classroom), or in a restricted set of settings (e.g., classrooms and playground of one school). Further, training is generally provided for a limited range of a particular response. However, in all but a few cases, the purpose of this training is to produce elaborated performance for a class of behaviors across a range of social settings. For instance, let us assume that "sharing" is included in a social skill intervention for 2nd-grade students. During intervention, students may be given opportunities to share balls, trucks, and blocks in an indoor play area. The intent of this training is to produce more generalized sharing—it would be desirable to observe participating students sharing academic materials, other toys, play equipment, or other materials in the classroom, lunch-

room, library, playground, or outside of school.

Thus, the efficiency and overall effectiveness of social interaction skills training will be increased by selecting target skills that represent more general response classes that occasion positive peer responses across a variety of social situations. In this way, slight variations of an individual skill can be more closely matched to the behavioral demands of a given situation, thus increasing the likelihood that a child's performance will produce reinforcing responses from peers.

3. *Select target behaviors that covary with specific social behaviors of peers.* Finally, we must select target behaviors that reliably follow specific peer initiations or precede positive peer responses. One major assumption of the entrapment model is that specific aspects of peers' social behavior can serve to prompt or reinforce the occurrence of desired social skills by children receiving training. In selecting target behaviors, then, we must give priority to those skills that are most likely to become "embedded" in social interactions with peers. To the extent that targeted social skills produce positive responses from peers, or to the extent that these behaviors are reliably prompted by peer behavior, the likelihood of entrapment is enhanced.

Thus, Kohler and Greenwood (1986) have offered *conceptual* guidelines for the selection of target behaviors in social interaction skills training. While we have not yet conducted much systematic research that explicitly follows these guidelines, a small collection of recent investigations does offer some further empirical guidance for planning interventions. Several of these investigations have been *descriptive,* using observational measures to compare and contrast the interactions of behaviorally handicapped and nonhandicapped children in naturalistic settings. Additionally, several *experimental* investigations have demonstrated differential effects for the entrapment of various target behaviors among young children. These investigations can serve as a solid empirical foundation for further research into the selection of target behaviors in social interaction skills training, and are briefly reviewed below.

Descriptive investigations. Descriptive studies based on observational assessment of children's social behavior offer one method for identifying specific skills that meet the multiple criteria for entrapment outlined above. Several investigations of this type have been completed with preschool children (e.g., Greenwood, Todd, Hops & Walker, 1982; Strain, 1983; Tremblay et al., 1981). Additionally, several investigations have examined relationships between observed social behaviors and sociometric status for nonhandicapped (e.g., Dodge, 1983) and handicapped (e.g., Bryan, 1974) elementary school children. To date, however, only a few studies have specifically examined social behavioral relationships between behaviorally handicapped children and their peers. Although these studies do not specifically address entrapment of social behavior, each has some relevance for the selection of target behaviors for intervention.

McConnell (1982) compared freeplay social behaviors of 43 handicapped and nonhandicapped boys in grades 1 through 4. Each handicapped subject received at least some educational services in regular education settings, and had been identified by his special education teacher as having difficulty making friends, playing appropriately, or being accepted by peers in mainstream settings.

The efficiency and overall effectiveness of social interaction skills training will be increased by selecting target skills that represent more general response classes that occasion positive peer responses across a variety of social situations.

> Participation in structured play activities must be assessed, and the frequency and type of social initiations made by children with disabilities, as well as peer responses to these initiations, must be examined more carefully.

Nonhandicapped participants were selected at random from regular education classrooms of the handicapped subjects.

McConnell found little difference in *broad* measures of social interaction for the two groups; handicapped and nonhandicapped boys spent similar amounts of time participating in some type of social play and talking with peers. Similarly, peers spoke to subjects in the two groups at equivalent rates.

However, several important differences emerged when more fine-grained measures were examined. First, handicapped children spent significantly less time than nonhandicapped peers in structured play (i.e., organized games). Second, handicapped children initiated to peers significantly *more* often than did nonhandicapped subjects. However, peers were less likely to respond to individual social initiations from handicapped subjects.

These findings suggest several general guidelines for the selection of target behaviors. First, participation in structured play activities must be assessed and, where necessary, brought to normative levels. Structured playground games appear to be a primary site for freeplay interaction among elementary school boys, and access to interaction during these games may facilitate entrapment of more specifically targeted social behaviors. Second, the frequency and type of social initiations made by handicapped children, as well as peer responses to these initiations, must be examined more carefully. Findings from McConnell's (1982) study indicated that handicapped subjects made more initiations than did nonhandicapped subjects, but engaged in equivalent overall rates of social interaction. Given that peers responded to a smaller proportion of initiations from handicapped subjects, one can wonder whether the specific social bids exhibited by these children differed in quality or type from the initiations of the nonhandicapped comparison group. Methods like those used by Tremblay et al. (1981), where peer responses to different types of social initiations were specifically evaluated, may aid in the further understanding of this effect.

In a second study, Foster and Ritchey (1985) observed children in grades 4 to 6 during two classroom activities. Observed children were assigned to one of three groups, based on positive and negative peer nomination sociometric assessment: accepted subjects (high number of positive nominations), rejected children (high number of negative nominations), and ignored children (few negative or positive nominations). Like McConnell's (1982) study, Foster and Ritchey found no differences in overall interaction rates for children in the three groups. However, observational assessment indicated that accepted children received more positive initiations from peers, and had a higher proportion of their total interactions initiated by peers (a measure of sociability from Greenwood et al., 1982) than subjects in either the rejected or neglected groups.

Across these two descriptive studies, several common findings emerge. Measures of discrete, child-specific behavior (e.g., subject initiations) may not discriminate behaviorally handicapped children from nonhandicapped peers.

Such differences do emerge, however, when one examines *relationships* between the social behavior of two or more children: handicapped students are more likely to be ignored following initiations to peers (McConnell, 1982), and are less likely to receive positive initiations from peers (Foster

& Ritchey, 1985). Thus, descriptive studies corroborate the notion that *interactive* variables may be relatively more important than discrete behavioral variables in the assessment, description, and treatment of social interaction deficits among elementary schoolaged children.

Experimental investigations. In addition to these correlational studies, two experimental investigations contribute to the identification of target behaviors that are likely to become entrapped. In the first, Walker, Greenwood, Hops, and Todd (1979) demonstrated that overall rates of social interaction for socially withdrawn elementary students changed as a function of specific components of interaction being reinforced by the teacher. Highest observed rates of social interaction occurred when children in a play group received praise *for continued interaction* with peers (i.e., a social initiation, followed by a positive response, followed by ongoing exchange of social behavior between two or more children). When children were praised for *only* initiations or responses, overall levels of social interaction declined. During these phases, subjects often engaged in what Walker and his colleagues termed "cocktail party" interactions—either a solitary initiation, or an initiation and response, followed by termination of the interaction. Thus, children produced and maintained high rates of social interaction only when reinforcement was contingent on the behavior of both interactants (i.e., continued interaction).

In a second experimental investigation, Kohler and Fowler (1985) demonstrated at least partial entrapment of one social skill among three elementary-aged girls. Subjects were trained to produce four specific types of social invitations (i.e., offer to share, offer assistance, inviting peers to play, requesting permission to play with peers); two subjects also received training in the use of social amenities (i.e., please, thank you, you're welcome, I'm sorry, or excuse me). Coaching procedures were introduced to increase rates of these target behaviors during freeplay activities with classmates, and rates of social invitations and amenities emitted by subjects and peers were recorded. These investigators focused on two particular types of peer responses: social reciprocity (i.e., the number of invitations or amenities directed to subject by peers) and social responsiveness (i.e., immediate acceptance or refusal of subject invitations).

For two of the children, Betty and Sarah, increased rates of social invitations to peers were associated with similar increases in rates of social invitations from peers. Although the third subject, Amanda, also increased her rate of invitations to peers, similar increases were *not* seen for peer invitations directed to her. Interestingly, both Betty and Sarah maintained their rates of social invitations to and from peers after termination of the initial intervention phase; sustained rates of social invitations were not noted for Amanda. Such maintenance was demonstrated only after the investigators introduced a group contingency to increase Amanda's peers' invitations to higher, more reciprocal rates.

Quite different effects were noted, however, for social amenities. Both Sarah and Betty increased their use of amenities during intervention. However, reciprocal increases were not obtained for peer social amenities directed to these subjects. Further, Betty's and Sarah's use of social amenities declined to baseline levels immediately following the withdrawal of intervention—no maintenance occurred.

> Descriptive studies corroborate the notion that *interactive* variables may be relatively more important than discrete behavioral variables in the assessment, description, and treatment of social interaction deficits among elementary school-aged children.

> Descriptive and experimental studies suggest the importance of a bidirectional perspective in assessment of social behavior for elementary students with behavioral disorders.

Kohler and Fowler (1985) thus conclude that peer reciprocity may contribute to the entrapment of social skills, and that such reciprocity may be relatively more important than social responsiveness, or more temporally related peer responses (e.g., positive response to social invitation). Further, these findings suggest that specific invitations to play are more likely to become entrapped, or maintained by naturally occurring peer behavior, than are verbal compliments and amenities.

Summary. Taken together, these descriptive and experimental studies suggest the importance of a bidirectional perspective in assessment of social behavior for elementary students with behavioral disorders. Interaction variables (e.g., responses from peers, ratios of initiations given to initiations received) more reliably discriminate behaviorally handicapped children from nonhandicapped classmates, and social behaviors associated with entrapment or changes in social interaction are more likely to be maintained or to generalize to nontreatment settings.

At this time, we know relatively little about interactional variables and possible entrapment effects in the social interactions of elementary schoolaged children; we know more about the social behavior of preschool children (Hops & Greenwood, in press; Kohler & Greenwood, 1986; Strain et al., 1984). However, several groups of investigators have recently begun to examine possible entrapment effects within *academic* interactions between elementary schoolaged children and their peers (Kohler, Greenwood, & Baer, 1985) or teachers (McConnell, Lenkner, Szumowski, & Strain, 1985). In both cases, researchers were able to produce new interaction patterns associated with increased rates of academic engagement. These recent analyses offer important parallels to work in child-child social interaction, and may possibly serve as prompts for continued work in this area.

Designing Intervention Procedures to Promote Entrapment

In addition to careful consideration in the selection of target behaviors, we may be able to promote the entrapment of social interaction skills through the use of specific intervention procedures. Generally, these procedures must be designed to initially increase rates of specific target behaviors through teacher-provided antecedents and/or consequences, and then remove these "artificial" elements of intervention in such a way that control over targeted skills is transferred to reinforcing elements of interaction with peers.

These treatment procedures must focus, to a large extent, on *the peer group* as the target for intervention. Rather than assuming that interactive difficulties are individual-specific and require change in some discrete target behavior, this analysis of entrapment suggests that treatment procedures directly target changes in interactions between the target child and his or her peers. Assume, for example, that observational measures indicate a 4th-grade child exhibits few positive initiations to peers and frequently responds negatively or aggressively to initiations from peers. Treatment based on a simple, individual-specific skill deficit model might include teacher praise and/or tokens to increase positive initiations to peers, and a response-cost program to decrease negative or aggressive responses; both elements of treatment would focus *solely* on the behavior of the referred child. An intervention to enhance entrapment may go further, however, to include direct reinforcement of *peer* behaviors associated with these targeted skills. For instance, a group contingency could be implemented whereby the entire play group is given access to additional freetime contingent on appropriate interaction rates of the referred child. In this way, both the target child and peers initially receive direct, teacher-provided reinforcement for increased rates of positive initiations (i.e., the child initiates, peer responds) and decreased rates of negative responses from the child; after initial implementation, this group contingency can be faded and control transferred to new, more positive interactive relationships between the behavior of the target child and peers. Thus, treatment effectiveness is enhanced by attention to changes in both target child and peer behavior.

Recently, increased attention has been devoted to group reinforcement contingencies (Greenwood & Hops, 1981) and other treatment procedures (Strain, 1981; Odom & Strain, 1984) that include *peers* in direct treatment of social behavioral excesses or deficits. These procedures hold particular promise for enhancing entrapment of adaptive social interaction for at least three reasons. First, group-oriented contingencies can be applied more effectively to *interactive* aspects of children's social behavior. In the example above, a group-oriented contingency was applied to increase rate of positive interactions initiated by the target child; thus, a single reinforcement program increased both the target child's rate of positive initiations to peers and the likelihood of peers' affirmative responses to these initations. Second, group-oriented contingencies and other peer-mediated interventions provide a framework for creating interactions that will ultimately lead to entrapment of targeted social responses. Finally, using group-oriented contingencies and other peer-mediated interventions enhances entrapment through the direct involvement of *peers* in the therapeutic process. Peers are expected to maintain entrapped social behaviors after treatment is terminated. As a result, the efficiency of intervention may be increased by including these peers as early as possible in the change program.

Group-oriented procedures that can be expected to enhance entrapment among elementary school students with behavioral disorders are currently available in three standardized, empirically validated social interaction skills intervention programs: RECESS (Reprograming Environmental Contingencies for Effective Social Skills; Walker et al., 1978), PEERS (Procedures for Establishing Effective Relationship Skills; Hops et al., 1978), and ACCEPTS (A Curriculum for Effective Peer and Teacher Skills; Walker et al., 1983). Each of these intervention packages includes, or has been adapted to include, treatment procedures that produce or enhance entrapment of adaptive social responding for behaviorally handicapped elementary school children. Each of these intervention packages and their respective entrapment procedures is described below.

RECESS. RECESS (Walker et al., 1978) is a comprehensive behavior management package designed to decrease negative/aggressive behavior and simultaneously increase positive, cooperative interaction of young elementary schoolaged children. RECESS is designed to be implemented primarily in playground settings, although the authors include procedures for extending program components to classroom or other situations. The intervention package includes four major components: (a) discrimination training, in which referred children are taught to

---

Treatment effectiveness is enhanced by attention to changes in both target child and peer behavior.

> The original developers of RECESS have carefully evaluated the effectiveness of individual treatment components and the overall treatment package.

identify appropriate versus inappropriate social behaviors: (b) a response-cost point system, implemented during daily freeplay activities to provide direct decelerative consequences for negative or aggressive behavior: (c) adult praise for positive and/or cooperative interaction during freeplay periods; and (d) concurrent group and individual reinforcement contingencies for child behavior during freeplay. As in many behavior change programs, this last reinforcement contingency provides points to the child contingent on daily performance; these points can be exchanged at home for one of several individual rewards. Additionally, the group-oriented contingency of this component provides the *entire classroom* with freetime activities contingent on the daily performance of the target child; in this way, peers receive direct reinforcement for participating in interactions where the child acquires, elaborates, or generalizes positive social behaviors.

The original developers of RECESS have carefully evaluated the effectiveness of individual treatment components and the overall treatment package (Walker et al., 1978; Walker, Hops, & Greenwood, 1984). Two particular findings are of relevance to the discussion here. First, Walker and his colleagues found that adult attention, particularly praise, was in and of itself insufficient to produce immediate or durable change in the behavior of socially negative or aggressive children; rather, the RECESS developers concluded that coercive interactions with peers, and ultimately the social behavior of these peers, was an important component in the maintenance of negative behavior by referred children. Second, field trails of RECESS suggested that group-oriented contingencies, in which classroom peers "shared" in the reinforcement of improved performance, increased the efficiency of the entire intervention package (Walker et al., 1978).

In a more recent investigation, RECESS intervention procedures were modified to increase peer involvement in ongoing treatment; as a result, we now have further evidence of possible entrapment effects with RECESS. Dougherty, Fowler, and Paine (1985) modified standard RECESS procedures by appointing and training peer monitors for recess intervention periods. These peer monitors observed the target child's behavior throughout recess, awarding points for positive or exemplary behavior and withdrawing points for negative behavior or violations of playground rules. These points were then exchanged, according to a prearranged criterion, for small group activities immediately following recess and for large group activities provided once each week. During peer monitoring treatment phases for Dennis, the first child treated, classmates served as peer monitors. Subsequently, Dennis served as peer monitor for Ed, the second child treated.

Peer monitors effectively maintained initial treatment effects obtained when a consultant operated the recess point system, and produced generalization to previously untreated periods for both Dennis and Ed. In all instances, negative interaction rates declined to near-zero levels following the introduction of treatment. In addition, Dougherty and her colleagues noted three other effects particularly relevant to the current discussion. First, Dennis' negative interactive behavior in an untreated recess period declined significantly to near-zero levels—following his appointment as Ed's peer monitor. Second, although Ed initially received treatment in only one of three daily recess periods, generalization occurred across two untreated periods. Finally, reductions in negative *peer* initiations to Dennis and Ed were observed with the onset of intervention. These reductions were similar to reductions to overall negative behavior for nontreated children following introduction of the peer monitoring condition.

Together, data offered by Walker et al. (1978) and Dougherty et al. (1985) demonstrate that RECESS produces changes in negative/social interaction that are likely to be entrapped through reinforcement during naturally occurring interactions with peers. Reduced levels of negative interaction and increased rates of positive interaction were maintained, at least to some extent, for several children in original field tests (Walker et al., 1978), and for both Dennis and Ed (Dougherty et al., 1985). Additionally, Dougherty and her colleagues noted generalization of intervention effects across untreated conditions, behaviors, and children in their investigation. Finally, it appears that RECESS implementors, particularly in the Dougherty investigation, successfully target behaviors for both acceleration and deceleration that are positively associated with social behaviors of peers. While the evidence for this final point is somewhat indirect, Dougherty and her colleagues document two important, concurrent changes: reduction in observed negative interaction rates for Dennis and Ed, accompanied by (a) application of simple peer monitoring procedures in which children monitored and provided feedback for the behavior of their classmates, and (b) reductions in negative peer initiations to the subjects as well as overall negative peer behavior during recess periods.

PEERS. PEERS (Hops et al., 1978) was developed by the same team responsible for RECESS, and was designed as a similarly comprehensive intervention package to increase the social interaction rates of socially withdrawn children in kindergarten through 3rd grade. PEERS contains four major program components: (a) social skills training, in which the referred child is taught and given opportunities to rehearse social initiations, responses to initiations, and strategies for continuing or extending interactions; (b) joint-task activities, in which the referred child and nonwithdrawn peers are given opportunities to interact during structured activities; (c) a reinforcement point system for social interaction during recess, where points earned by the child are exchanged for classwide activities; and (d) a correspondence training procedure, in which the child is taught to describe accurately social behavior occurring during preceding recess periods, so that classroom teachers can provide additional reinforcement. As with RECESS, the PEERS reinforcement point system includes an interdependent group contingency—reinforcement for the peer group is provided contingent on the behavior of one child (i.e., the child receiving treatment), with peers "contributing" to points earned by interacting with the child. In this way, PEERS explicitly establishes and then systematically fades an artificial reinforcement contingency that is designed to promote entrapment of social interaction.

Paine and his colleagues (1982) evaluated the effects of brief, repeated "booster sessions" of PEERS intervention procedures on subsequent maintenance of increased rates of social interaction. Earlier work (reported by Baer and Wolf, 1970) had suggested that repeated exposure to brief (e.g., 3 to 5 day) periods of intervention leads to maintenance of higher rates of social interaction. Paine's group sought to

---

PEERS was developed by the same team responsible for RECESS, and was designed as a similarly comprehensive intervention package to increase the social interaction rates of socially withdrawn children in kindergarten through 3rd grade.

> ACCEPTS was designed to teach critical social skills to children with mild and moderate disabilities prior to their full-time integration into regular education settings.

replicate and extend this earlier work, evaluating the relative effects of repeated intervention for subjects who had either completed intervention earlier or were being exposed to intervention for the first time.

Participating in this study were 9 elementary-aged, socially withdrawn children; 5 of the children had completed PEERS treatment 1 to 6 months prior to this investigation, and had returned to low levels of interaction with peers. The remaining 4 subjects had not received any treatment for social withdrawal prior to their participation in this project. All participants received three 5-day sessions of intervention, interspersed with baseline periods in which no intervention was provided. Intervention included the recess-based point system, social skills training, joint tasks, and correspondence training as originally outlined in PEERS (Hops et al., 1978).

All subjects immediately and significantly increased their rates of social interaction during each intervention period. Additionally, 5 of the 9 children (4 of whom had previously received treatment) showed increased maintenance over the courses of the study. While reversals were noted for interaction rates following each withdrawal of treatment, the extent of these reversals declined across booster sessions. By the end of the third intervention period, all 5 children were interacting at normative rates in the *absence* of explicit, teacher mediated reinforcement. For these children, social interaction had come under the control of naturally occurring reinforcers.

ACCEPTS. ACCEPTS (Walker et al., 1983) was designed to teach critical social skills to mildly and moderately handicapped children prior to their full-time integration into regular education settings. Three major components make up ACCEPTS: (a) social skills training, a small-group instructional arrangement in which children are taught to produce 24 different skills for interacting with peers in freeplay settings, and 4 skills for interacting with teachers in academic settings; (b) recess coaching, which combines adult-mediated prompts and praise with a group-oriented contingency management system to increase the use of critical social skills during child-child interaction; and (c) a classroom-based, individual specific contingency management program to increase a child's appropriate interactions with teachers and overall adjustment to the demands of the classroom setting.

ACCEPTS draws heavily on procedures thought to facilitate entrapment. To the maximum extent possible, target behaviors for the social skills training sequence were selected that were empirically associated with (a) positive responses from peers, (b) appropriate interaction, or (c) more general measures of peer preference and social competence. Further, social skills training lessons were designed to lead children to mastery in the performance of specific skills *prior* to exposing these skills to reinforcement contingencies in freeplay activities; in this way, children are more likely to produce social responses of sufficient quality that peers are more likely to respond. Finally, nonhandicapped peers from the target child's regular education class are included in social skills training lessons and recess coaching. In this way, peers can both provide positive models for the target child, and can begin to develop new skills for interacting with that child in a wide variety of settings.

In one of the initial evaluations of the ACCEPTS program (McConnell & Walker, 1983; Walker et al., 1983), the effects of social skills training and recess coaching on a small set of "critical skills" was evaluated. These skills included positive initiations to peers, positive responses to peer initiations, compliments, smiles, and touches, and were selected on an a *priori* basis as being essential components for a more general measure of social interaction.

Randomly assigned to treatment or control groups were 20 mildly handicapped second to fifth grade students, identified by their teachers as lacking essential social skills. Children in the treatment group received the total ACCEPTS intervention package, including small group social skills training, recess coaching, and classroom contingency management in regular education classrooms; children in the control group received only those services already available in their resource rooms. Observations were conducted for all subjects prior to, during, and after a 6-week intervention period. Results indicated that children receiving treatment significantly increased their rates of positive "entrapment skills" during intervention, and that this increased rate was maintained at slightly lower levels following the termination of treatment. Unfortunately, these data represent group means, and are based on observations completed several weeks apart. As a result, it is difficult to describe specific changes in the interactions of these children over the course of intervention or to offer more detailed information on the mechanisms by which this maintenance was obtained.

Summary. RECESS, PEERS, and ACCEPTS each appear to incorporate intervention procedures associated with entrapment of social interaction skills for elementary school students with behavioral handicaps. Each of these intervention programs was originally designed, and in one case has been further adapted, to specifically include peers in the ongoing treatment of social behavior excesses or deficits. Inclusion of peers leads directly to changes in child-child interaction that are likely to support more adaptive interaction long after intervention is ended.

To some extent, maintenance effects associated with each of these intervention programs offers tentative evidence that new, more adaptive responses of behaviorally handicapped children are coming under the control of naturally occurring, peer-mediated reinforcers. However, as Kohler and Greenwood (1986) have shown, maintenance of behavior change is but one part of a more complete proof for the existence of entrapment. Future research, particularly more detailed analyses of changes in child-child interactions during any or all of these interventions, can be expected to more clearly describe the processes of entrapment, as well as to increase the efficiency and effectiveness of social behavioral interventions with children.

CONCLUSION

Children are referred for social skills training because, at least in part, they fail to demonstrate competence in their interactions with peers. Historically, these problems have been conceptualized as social skill deficits: The child does not exhibit specific skills (e.g., social initiations), or does not exhibit these skills at appropriate frequencies. However, social interaction is a reciprocal, bidirectional process. As a result, changes in the social behavior of one child may often require changes in the associated social behavior of others, such as peers in a child's class.

Entrapment is a process through which the social behavior of one child comes under the control of naturally occurring reinforcers. In

> Changes in the social behavior of one child may often require changes in the associated social behavior of others, such as peers in a child's class.

particular, entrapment can occur when changes in the social behavior of one child are reinforced by the social behavior of others during interactions in naturalistic settings. When this type of entrapment occurs, we expect newly-acquired social behaviors to continue at high rates and to generalize to new settings or behaviors long after intervention is terminated.

To produce this entrapment of more adaptive social skills, we must pay particular attention to both the selection of target behaviors and the use of intervention tactics that reflect the interactive nature of child-child social behavior; in particular, we must work to create social interactions that naturally provide reinforcement for the continued use and elaboration of recently acquired skills. As such, emphasis on entrapment leads to a reconceptualization for our definition of social skills training.

Research on entrapment effects in social skills assessment and training with behaviorally handicapped elementary school students is clearly in its infancy. At this point, we have some evidence that entrapment occurs (e.g., Baer & Wolf, 1970; Dougherty et al., 1985; Kohler & Greenwood, 1986). However, continued systematic inquiry is still needed to more fully describe the process of entrapment, and to more carefully include procedures that foster this process in our social behavior interventions. The results of this research can be expected to dramatically increase the power and efficiency of interventions for children with behavioral handicaps.

REFERENCES

Baer, D. M., & Wolf, M. M. (1970). The entry into natural communities of reinforcement. In R. Ulrich, T. Stachnik, & J. Mabry (Eds.), *Control of human behavior.* Glenview, IL: Scott-Foresman.

Bornstein, M., Bellack, A. S., & Hersen, M. (1980). Social skills training for highly aggressive children: Treatment in an inpatient psychiatric setting. *Behavior Modification, 4,* 173-186.

Bryan, T. H. (1974). An observational analysis of classroom behavior of children with learning disabilities. *Journal of Learning Disabilities, 7(10),* 26-34.

Cartledge, G., & Milburn, J. (1980). *Teaching social skills to children: Innovative approaches.* New York: Pergamon.

Charlesworth, R., & Hartup, W. W. (1967). Positive social reinforcement in the nursery school play group. *Child Development, 38,* 993-1002.

Dodge, K. A. (1983). Behavioral antecedents of peer social status. *Child Development, 51,* 162-170.

Dougherty, B. S., Fowler, S. A., & Paine, S. C. (1985). The use of peer monitors to reduce negative interaction during recess. *Journal of Applied Behavior Analysis, 18,* 141-153.

Foster, S. L., & Ritchey, W. L. (1979). Issues in the assessment of social competence in children. *Journal of Applied Behavior Analysis, 12,* 625-638.

Foster, S. L., & Ritchey, W. L. (1985). Behavioral correlates of sociometric status of fourth-, fifth-, and sixth-grade children in two classroom settings. *Behavioral Assessment, 7,* 79-93.

Green, K. D., Vosk, B., Forehand, R., Beck, S. J., & Vosk, B. (1980). An assessment of the relationship between measures of children's social competence and children's academic achievement. *Child Development, 51,* 1149-1156.

Greenwood, C. R., & Hops, H. (1981). Group-oriented contingencies and peer behavior change. In P. S. Strain (Ed.), *The utilization of classroom peers as behavior change agents* (pp. 189-259). New York: Plenum.

Greenwood, C. R., Todd, N. M., Hops, H., & Walker, H. M. (1982). Behavior change targets in the assessment and modification of socially withdrawn preschool children. *Behavioral Assessment, 4,* 273-297.

Gresham, F. M. (1986). Conceptual and definitional issues in the assessment

---

> Emphasis on entrapment leads to a reconceptualization for our definition of social skills training.

of children's social skills: Implications for classification and treatment. *Journal of Clinical Child Psychology, 15,* 3-15.

Hartup, W. W. (1983). The peer system. In P. H. Mussen (Series Ed.) and E. M. Hetherington (Vol. Ed.), *Handbook of child psychology* (4th ed.): *Vol. 4. Socialization, personality, and social development* (pp. 103-196). New York: Wiley.

Hops, H. (1982). Social skills training for socially isolated children. In P. Karoly & J. Steffen (Eds.), *Enhancing children's social competencies.* Lexington, MA: Lexington Books.

Hops, H., Finch, M., & McConnell, S. (1985). Social skills deficits. In P. H. Bornstein & A. E. Kazdin (Eds.), *Handbook of clinical behavior therapy with children* (pp. 543-598). Homewood, IL: Dorsey.

Hops, H., & Greenwood, C. R. (1981). Social skills deficits. In E. J. Mash & L. G. Terdal (Eds.), *Behavioral assessment of childhood disorders.* New York: Guilford.

Hops, H., & Greenwood, C. R. (in press). Social skills deficits. In E. J. Mash & L. G. Terdal (Eds.), *Behavioral assessment of childhood disorders* (2nd ed.). New York: Guilford.

Hops, H., Guild, J. J., Fleischman, D. H., Paine, S. C., Street, A., Walker, H. M., & Greenwood, C. R. (1978). *PEERS (Procedures for Establishing Effective Relationship Skills): Manual for consultants.* Unpublished manuscript, University of Oregon, Center at Oregon for Behavioral Education of the Handicapped, Eugene.

Kauffman, J. M. (1985). *Characteristics of children's behavior disorders* (3rd ed.). Columbus, OH: Merrill.

Kohler, F. W., & Fowler, S. A. (1985). Training prosocial behaviors to young children: An analysis of reciprocity with untrained peers. *Journal of Applied Behavior Analysis, 18,* 187-200.

Kohler, F. W., & Greenwood, C. R. (1986). Toward a technology of generalization: The identification of natural contingencies of reinforcement. *The Behavior Analyst, 9,* 19-26.

Kohler, F. W., Greenwood, C. R., & Baer, D. M. (1985, May). *Assessing the peer tutoring process: The identification of natural communities of social reinforcement.* Paper presented at the annual meeting of the Association of Behavior Analysis, Columbus, OH.

McConnell, S. R. (1982). *Identification of social skills for handicapped boys: Evaluation of teacher rating, peer sociometric, and direct observation measures.* Unpublished doctoral dissertation, University of Oregon.

McConnell, S. R., Lenkner, D. A., Szumowski, E., & Strain, P. S. (1985, May). *Effects of child academic behavior on rates of contingent teacher attention: Entry into a complex community of reinforcement.* Paper presented at the annual meeting of the Association for Behavior Analysis, Columbus, OH.

McConnell, S. R., Strain, P. S., Kerr, M. M., Stagg, V., Lenkner, D. A., & Lambert, D. L. (1984). An empirical definition of school adjustment: Selection of target behaviors for a comprehensive treatment program. *Behavior Modification, 8,* 451-473.

McConnell, S. R., & Walker, H. M. (1983, May). *Peer-mediated behavior change within a standardized social skills curriculum.* Paper presented at the annual meeting of the Association for Behavior Analysis, Milwaukee, WI.

Odom, S. L., & Strain, P. S. (1984). Peer-mediated approaches to increasing children's social interactions: A review. *American Journal of Orthopsychiatry, 54,* 544-557.

Paine, S. C., Hops, H., Walker, H. M., Greenwood, C. R., Fleischman, D. H., & Guild, J. J. (1982). Repeated treatment effects: A study of maintaining behavior change in socially withdrawn children. *Behavior Modification, 6,* 171-199.

Patterson, G. R. (1982). *Coercive family processes.* Eugene, OR: Castalia.

Schloss, P. J., Schloss, C. N., Wood, C. E., & Kiehl, W. S. (1986). A critical review of social skills research with behaviorally disordered students. *Behavioral Disorders, 12,* 1-14.

Stokes, T. F., & Baer, D. M. (1977). An implicit technology of generalization. *Journal of Applied Behavior Analysis, 9,* 349-367.

Stokes, T. F., & Osnes, P. G. (1986). Programming for the generalization of children's social behavior. In P. S. Strain, M. J. Guralnick, & H. M. Walker (Eds.), *Children's social behavior: Development, assessment,* and modification. Orlando, FL: Academic Press.

Strain, P. S. (Ed.). (1981). *The utilization of classroom peers as behavior change agents.* New York: Plenum.

Strain, P. S. (1983). Identification of social skill curriculum targets for severely handicapped children in mainstream preschools. *Applied Research in Mental Retardation, 4,* 369-382.

Strain, P. S., Odom, S. L., & McConnell, S. R. (1984). Promoting social reciprocity of exceptional children: Identification, target behavior selection, and intervention. *Remedial and Special Education, 5,* 21-28.

Strain, P. S., & Shores, R. E. (1977). Social reciprocity: Review of research and educational implications. *Exceptional Children, 43,* 526-531.

Tremblay, A., Strain, P. S., Hendrickson, J. M., & Shores, R. E. (1981). Social interactions of normally developing preschool children: Using normative data for subject and target behavior selection. *Behavior Modification, 5,* 237-253.

Van Hasselt, V. B., Hersen, M., Whitehall, M. B., & Bellack, A. S. (1979). Social skills assessment and training with children: An evaluative review. *Behavior Research and Therapy, 17,* 413-437.

Walker, H. M., Greenwood, C. R., Hops, H., & Todd, N. M. (1979). Differential effects of reinforcing topographic components of social interaction: Analysis and systematic replication. *Behavior Modification, 3,* 291-321.

Walker, H. M., Hops, H., & Greenwood, C. R. (1984). The CORBEH research and development model: Programmatic issues and strategies. In S. C. Paine, G. T. Bellamy, & B. Wilcox (Eds.), *Human services that work: From innovation to standard practice* (pp. 57-77). Baltimore, MD: Brookes.

Walker, H. M., McConnell, S. R., & Clarke, J. Y. (1985). Social skills training in school settings: A model for the social integration of handicapped children in less restrictive settings. In R. J. McMahon & R. DeV. Peters (Eds.), *Childhood disorders: Behavioral-developmental approaches.* New York: Bruner-Mazel.

Walker, H. M., McConnell, S. R., Walker, J., Holmes, D., Todis, B., & Golden, N. (1983). *ACCEPTS: A Curriculum for Effective Peer and Teacher Skills.* Austin, TX: Pro-Ed.

Walker, H. M., Street, A., Garrett, B., Crossen, J., Hops, H., & Greenwood, C. R. (1978). *RECESS (Reprograming Environmental Contingencies for Effective Social Skills): Manual for consultants.* Unpublished manuscript, University of Oregon, Center at Oregon for Behavioral Education of the Handicapped, Eugene.

Warrenfeltz, R. B., Kelly, W. J., Salzberg, C. L., Beegle, C. P., Levy, S. M., Adams, T. A., & Crouse, T. R. (1981). Social skills training of behavior disordered adolescents with self-monitoring to promote generalization to a vocational setting. *Behavioral Disorders, 7,* 18-27.

Structured Learning Using Self-Monitoring to Promote Maintenance and Generalization of Social Skills Across Settings for a Behaviorally Disordered Adolescent

Cheryl Strobel Kiburz
Sidney R. Miller
Lonny W. Morrow

ABSTRACT: Recent literature has highlighted the importance of teaching social skills to behaviorally disordered adolescents. Although it has been demonstrated that social skills can be taught to this population, skills maintenance and generalization have remained problematic. Using a multiple baseline-across-behaviors design, the present investigation incorporated techniques designed to facilitate maintenance and generalization of skills. This study involved an 18-year-old youth placed in a residential state mental health facility because of social skills deficits that included greetings, initiating conversation, and thanking behavior. The treatment occurred over a 48-day period in which the student was observed in four distinct settings. Results suggest that the skills trained—greetings and thanking behavior—were maintained and generalized to three natural settings: (a) the route the student walked to the classroom, (b) the student lounge located near the classroom, and (c) a vocational setting located within walking distance of the classroom. Training also produced an incidental increase in the skill initiating conversation.

Reprinted from *Behavioral Disorders*, Vol. 10, Number 1, November 1984, pp. 47-55.

With the increased emphasis on vocational training and community placement, the need to teach appropriate social skills to behaviorally disordered adolescents is becoming essential. As Adams, Strain, Salzberg, and Levy (1979) observed, social skills are necessary in those settings in which individuals are required to interact with others (e.g., school, work, and community). Failure in job placement is often linked to poor social-interpersonal skills rather than inadequate specific job skills (Kochany & Keller, 1980). In all, a growing body of literature substantiates the fact that social skills are imperative for successful employment of behaviorally disordered adolescents (Foss & Peterson, 1981).

There have been a variety of approaches used to teach social skills to nonhandicapped and handicapped populations. Studies have tested the effects of manipulating antecedents (Ballard, Corman, Gottlieb, & Kaufman, 1978; Shores, Hester, & Strain, 1976; Strain & Timm, 1974), consequences (Buell, Stoddard, Harris, & Baer, 1968; Mayhew, Enyart, &

> One method to promote maintenance and generalization is the use of self-monitoring.

Anderson, 1978; Walker, Greenwood, Hops, & Todd, 1979), the use of modeling (Marburg, Houston, & Holmes, 1976; O'Connor, 1969, 1972), and cognitive behavioral techniques (Gresham & Nagle, 1980; Meichenbaum, 1977; Zahavi & Asher, 1978). Further, Goldstein, Sprafkin, Gershaw, and Klein (1983) reported a structured learning strategy as effective in training social skills with a wide variety of populations including those described as aggressive, withdrawn, immature, or developmentally delayed. However, in spite of the effectiveness of these procedures for promoting skills acquisition, few studies have demonstrated maintenance and generalization of the skills trained (Gresham, 1981).

One method being investigated to promote maintenance and generalization is the use of self-monitoring (O'Leary & Dubey, 1979) in which an individual is responsible for systematically monitoring and recording his/her own performance of certain behaviors (Workman, 1982). For example, self-monitoring procedures were incorporated in treatments designed to increase both academic and social behavior (Turkewitz, O'Leary, & Ironsmith, 1975) and in social skills training programs (Warrenfeltz, Kelly, Salzberg, Beegle, Levy, Adams, & Crouse, 1981). Turkewitz et al. (1975) combined a modified token program with self-monitoring to increase academic and social behavior of eight disruptive youth. The skills were not generalized to a new setting and maintenance was observed only in the regular classroom across subject areas. In the Warrenfeltz et al. (1981) study, four behaviorally disordered adolescents participated in a vocationally oriented social skills training program. The first procedure consisted of didactic instruction and resulted in no concomitant change in most of the student's interpersonal behavior in the generalization setting (i.e., vocational training room). A subsequent intervention, role-playing and self-monitoring, was implemented and the targeted social skills generalized to the vocational training site. However, since the role-play and the self-monitoring procedure were implemented simultaneously, their separate effects could not be isolated and measured. These findings suggest that self-monitoring facilitates maintenance and generalization of social skills trained following termination of the intervention. Further research is needed to replicate these results and extricate the individual contributions of each treatment component.

The present study investigated the separate effects of structured learning (using modeling, role-playing, and performance feedback) and self-monitoring procedures on promoting maintenance and generalization of social skills across settings with a severely behaviorally disordered adolescent.

METHODOLOGY

Subject

The subject was an 18-year-old Caucasian male resident of a mental health and development center located in southern Illinois. He was admitted to the center at the age of 15. His behavior at admission consisted of aggressive acts (e.g., striking others and damaging property), chronic bizarre behaviors (e.g., eating soap, drinking shampoo), yelling and cursing for no apparent reason, and poor peer and staff interactions. A 3-year-old psychological evaluation reported him as mildly retarded based on an IQ of 60 (WAIS-R). A recent psychological reported identified the student as too emotionally disturbed to submit to standardized testing. He received daily instruction in reading, mathematics, spelling, writing, domestic, and vocational skills in classroom and vocational settings.

Settings

The study was conducted in four different settings. Social skills instruction occurred in a classroom that served five other seriously behaviorally disordered adolescents. Small group instruction was provided by a female, certified special education teacher. Generalization probes took place in three settings: (a) the route the student walked to the classroom, (b) the student lounge located near the classroom, and (c) a vocational setting located within walking distance of the classroom.

Behavioral Definitions

Behaviors selected for intervention were based on the results of subjective evaluation, a procedure with established precedent in naturalistic settings (Kazdin, 1982). This process consisted of obtaining opinions of persons knowledgeable about the behavior patterns of behaviorally disordered persons and/or who were familiar with the student. Specifically, the classroom teacher, program manager, supervisor, and classroom aide were asked to evaluate the student's social skills and to prioritize those in need of immediate remediation. Following identification of those social skills to be trained (e.g., greetings, thankings, and initiating conversation), criteria to score each appropriate social behavior were defined (see Appendix).

Assessment

Before training was initiated, baseline data were gathered to determine the number of behaviors the student (a) was able to verbalize for each targeted response, and (b) could perform for each targeted response. To determine the student's existing repertoire of social behavior, he was asked to discuss the steps to perform the targeted skills. Second, his ability to perform the targeted skills was assessed by presenting situations similar to real life that required him to perform the targeted skills. Training continued until he had achieved 100% mastery and performance was stable in both assessment areas. No feedback or reinforcement for correct answers or performance was provided.

Assessment data were gathered continuously at the three generalization sites (i.e., the route the student walked to the classroom, the student lounge, and the vocational setting) for 20 min daily. Trained observers recorded the appropriate or inappropriate performance of each targeted skill. Since the data gathered at the generalization sites were collected in settings not subject to examiner control, the frequency of opportunities to exhibit the behavior varied according to the social situation. To reflect the proportion of appropriate responses to the number of opportunities to respond over time, percentage measures were obtained by counting both the number of opportunities for the behavior to occur and the number of appropriate responses, and then dividing that count by the total opportunities (Gentry & Haring, 1976). A percentage scale was utilized to equalize the data (Repp, 1979).

Training

Training took place in the classroom during 30-min sessions of structured learning consisting of four major components: (a) modeling, (b) role-playing, (c) performance feedback, and (d) transfer of training; these are described as follows:

Modeling. Teaching the social skill began by exposing the subject, within a small group, to controlled appropriate examples of the skill being

> Social skills instruction occurred in a classroom that served five other adolescents with serious behavioral disorders.

> A multiple baseline design across skills combined with withdrawal features was employed to evaluate intervention effectiveness and response maintenance.

exhibited by the teacher. Each skill was taught separately and the modeling process depicted several examples of the skill used in different situations. To make the presentations as concrete as possible, the skill was broken down into component behavioral steps and illustrated in the modeling.

Role-playing. Following the presentation of modeling, a group discussion ensued. The group was urged to comment on what they saw and heard and to relate the behaviors to their own lives. From the information generated in the discussions, role-plays were developed. Each student was given the opportunity to role-play or practice the skills taught as a rehearsal for situations similar to real life. The student then had the opportunity to be the principle model and re-enact the modeled skill. During the role-play, support and coaching were provided.

Performance feedback. Following the role-play, the teacher elicited performance feedback (i.e., praise, compliments, approval, constructive criticism) from the group members. In this component, the student was given support as well as constructive suggestions for improving his performance.

Transfer of training. In the classroom setting, structured social learning included modeling, role-playing, and performance feedback instruction. Self-monitoring was implemented in a later phase to determine the separate effects of this instructional technique on maintenance and generalization across settings. The student was taught the skill of self-monitoring in the same fashion as the targeted social skills. The trainer began by modeling self-monitoring, followed by role-playing and performance feedback. The student was then provided a self-monitoring form. The trainer asked the student to take the self-monitoring form with him at the beginning of each day and to record, by circling a number, each time he performed the targeted skill appropriately. The student used self-monitoring at each generalization site. Staff members were informed that the student would be monitoring his own behavior at these specified sites. He was asked to bring his monitoring form to the subsequent classroom where it was discussed. He received social reinforcement for returning and completing the form.

Next, a reinforcement contingency was added to the self-monitoring procedure based on a reinforcement survey that revealed tangible reinforcers and social activities, such as going to a local restaurant, were the most reinforcing events. In this phase, the student continued the same self-monitoring procedure, but this time the forms were discussed in an evaluative manner with points assigned according to the number of times he performed the skill appropriately. A changing criterion for the number of points to be accumulated during each period of time was imposed according to his previous performance.

Evaluation Design

A multiple baseline design across skills combined with withdrawal features was employed to evaluate intervention effectiveness and response maintenance (Rusch & Kazdin, 1981). Intervention began with the first three components of the structured learning approach, followed by the fourth component, transfer of training, which in this study was self-monitoring. Next, self-monitoring with reinforcement was implemented, followed again by self-monitoring and then a return to baseline conditions.

Reliability

Two college students served as observers and were trained simultaneously and independently to observe targeted social skills in role-play situations similar to real life. Interobserver agreement was calculated by dividing the larger number of appropriate responses by the smaller and multiplying by 100 to provide a percentage score. This method has been labeled the *Whole Session Method* (Repp, 1979).

RESULTS

Reliability in the generalization settings was assessed at least once a week throughout the study (12 days), and was based on a mark-by-mark comparison of data collected by the two observers. The mean interobserver agreement for the skill greeting was 87% (range 83-100%); for thanking, 90% (range 75-100%); while for conversation it was 97% (range 80-100%).

During the baseline condition, the student's behavior was characterized by low mean percentages of appropriate social skills at the generalization settings. The mean percentage ranged from 13-41% for greetings, 8-24% for thankings, and 40-57% for initiating conversation, respectively.

Training began by employing three components of the structured learning process (modeling, role-playing, and performance feedback) for each skill. The student received training on each targeted skill until he was able to verbalize the steps with 100% accuracy and performance was stable. He was also required to role-play the appropriate use of the skill in different situations with 100% accuracy. The student required eight sessions to reach criterion for each skill, for both knowing the behavioral components and performing the skill in role-play situations. During this phase, the student's mean percentage of appropriate skills also increased when compared to baseline condition; ranging between 49-61% for greeting, 32-57% for thanking, and 53-67% for initiating conversation, respectively.

Following the training phase a self-monitoring phase, in which the student was taught self-monitoring utilizing the same procedure used to teach the targeted social skills, was implemented. Training continued until 90% criterion was met and stable. He reached criterion in four self-monitoring sessions involving greeting and in two self-monitoring sessions involving thanking. As before, during this phase the student performed the skills appropriately with mean percentages ranging from 51-63% for greeting, 48-70% for thanking, and 62-70% for initiating conversation.

The next phase included a reinforcement contingency added to the self-monitoring procedure. The range of mean percentages for performance for greetings were 71-89%; for thanking, 58-100%; while for initiating conversation, they were 69-97% across settings.

Following self-monitoring with reinforcement, a return to self-monitoring was implemented. The student maintained a higher mean percentage of appropriate skill performance than the training phase but the mean percentages of appropriate performance did decrease from the self-monitoring with reinforcement phase (see Figures 1 and 2). The mean percentages of this phase ranged from 71-77% for greeting, 64-79% for thanking, and 77-84% for initiating conversation.

The final phase included a return to baseline in which a higher mean percentage of appropriate social

> The student received training on each targeted skill until he was able to verbalize the steps with 100% accuracy and performance was stable.

> The effects of structured learning and self-monitoring were isolated and measured to determine their impact on the maintenance and generalization of social skills trained.

skills compared to preceding phases of the study was evidenced. Data were available for greeting only because of changes in the student's daily schedule. The mean percentage of appropriate performance of greeting ranged from 91-95%.

Generalization data are presented on the route the student walked to the educational center (Figure 1), the student lounge (Figure 2), and the vocational center (Figure 3), respectively. (The figures display the percentage of appropriate performance of each skill according to the number of opportunities provided in the natural setting.) The figures show that the student's generalization performance was greatest when self-monitoring was paired with reinforcement. When reinforcement was withdrawn and only self-monitoring was utilized, the student's generalization performance maintained at a higher mean percentage compared to the baseline condition.

DISCUSSION

This study sought to expand on the earlier studies of Turkewitz et al. (1975) and Warrenfletz et al. (1981). Unlike these investigations which utilized a combination of procedures to increase appropriate social behavior, in this study the effects of structured learning and self-monitoring were isolated and measured to determine their impact on the maintenance and generalization of social skills trained. In addition, the effectiveness of self-monitoring procedures combined with reinforcement was explored.

The structured learning process (modeling, role-playing, and performance feedback) resulted in a rapid acquisition of new social skills. Although generalization of social skills to other settings occurred, it was at a lesser extent than occurred when self-monitoring was implemented. The greatest level of appropriate performance was reached when self-monitoring with reinforcement was utilized. Withdrawal of treatment resulted in the maintenance of social skills taught at a higher level than was attained prior to training, but a lesser level than reached during the reinforcement and self-monitoring phases.

The similarity of data points between the two skills of greeting and initiating conversation is noteworthy. Although no interventions were implemented for the skill initiating conversation, the interventions implemented for greeting apparently had an effect on this skill. This similarity may have been, in part, the result of the overlap of these two social behaviors.

Before implementing the self-monitoring phase of the study, researchers had briefly informed staff members at the three generalization settings about the social skills being taught and also explained the self-monitoring process. Although cooperative, in future studies it would be beneficial to provide training to staff members at these sites. The training should consist of the following components: (a) instruction on the behavioral steps of the skills trained, (b) training of how to model the skill appropriately, and (c) instruction in how to provide social reinforcement to the student for appropriate performance of the skill. Training of personnel would provide continuity of expectations across generalization settings and might facilitate the generalization of appropriate performance of the skill.

In applied research, ideal opportunities for data collection are not always available due to the variability of conditions in naturalistic settings. This study was limited in

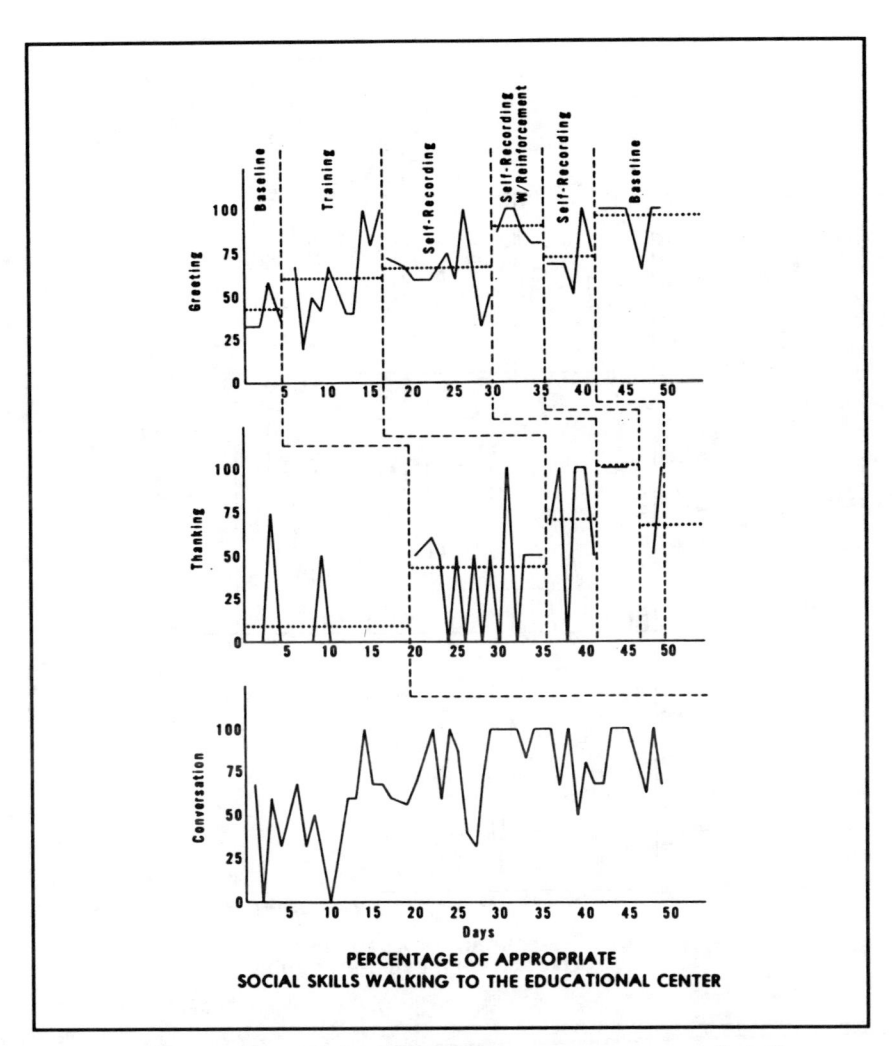

Figure 1. Percentage of greeting, thanking, and conversational skills displayed while walking to the educational center.

terms of an ability to control antecedent conditions during data collection phases of the project. For this reason, data were converted to percentages based upon student response in relationship to opportunity to respond, allowing for a more accurate assessment of student performance, facilitating monitoring of student progress, and interpretation of final results. Still, Cooper (1981) has cautioned that percentage data should be interpreted judiciously to avoid overrepresentation.

Future studies are necessary to determine the consistency of effects across different subjects and across a broader range of targeted social skills. Finally, it would be beneficial to measure the generalization and maintenance of the targeted social behaviors in a wider array of environmental settings.

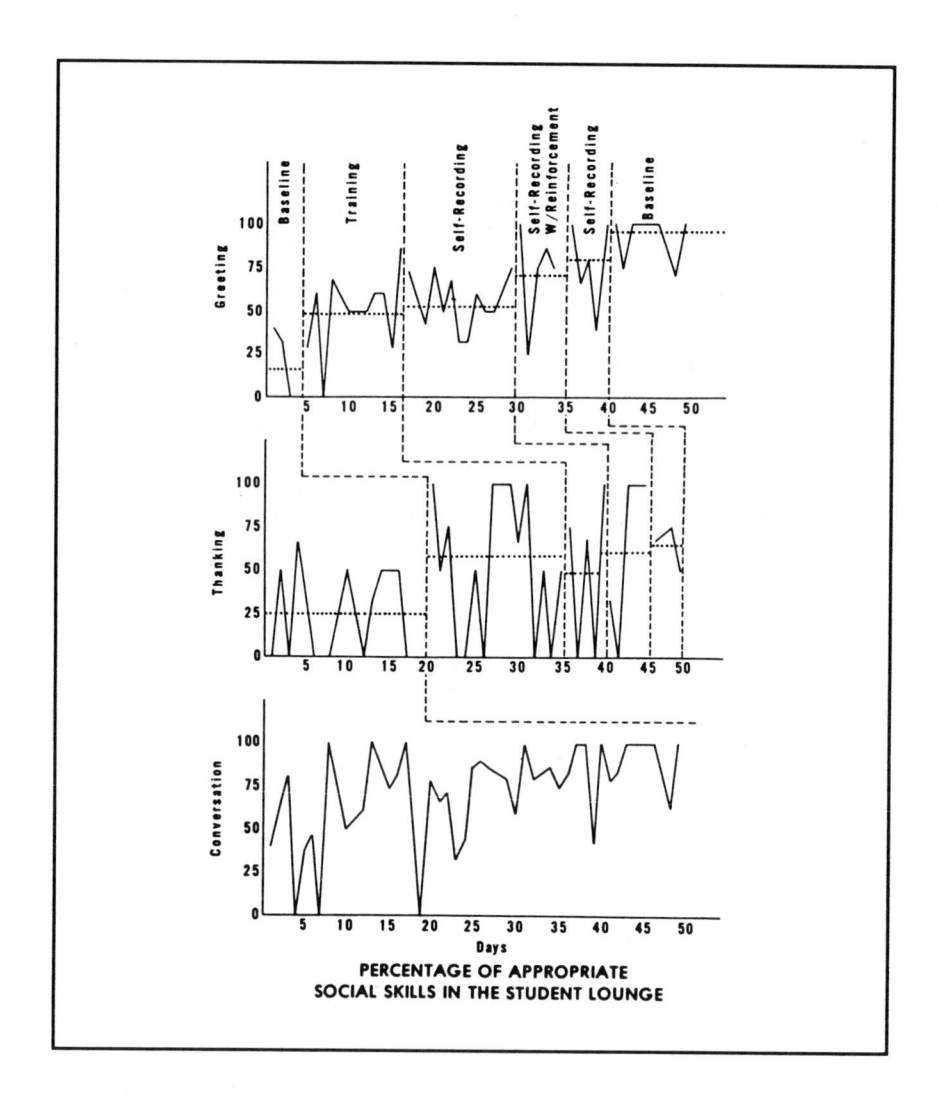

Figure 2. Percentage of greeting, thanking, and conversational skills displayed in the student lounge.

REFERENCES

Adams, T. W., Strain, P. S., Salzberg, C. L., & Levy, S. (1979). A model program for prevocational/vocational education with moderately and severely handicapped adolescents. *Journal of Special Education Technology, 3,* 36-42.

Ballard, M., Corman, L., Gottlieb, J., & Kaufman, M. J. (1978). Improving the social status of mainstreamed retarded children. *Journal of Education Psychology, 69,* 605-611.

Buell, J., Stoddard, P., Harris, F. R., & Baer, D. M. (1968). Collateral social development accompanying reinforcement of outdoor in a preschool child. *Journal of Applied Behavior Analysis, 1,* 167-173.

Cooper, J. O. (1981). *Measuring behavior* (2nd ed.). Columbus, OH: Charles E. Merrill.

Foss, G., & Peterson, S. L. (1981). Social interpersonal skills relevant to job tenure for mentally retarded adults. *Mental Retardation, 19,* 103-106.

Gentry, D., & Haring, N. (1976). Essentials of performance measurement. In N. G. Haring & L. J. Brown (Eds.), *Teaching the severely handicapped* (Vol. 1). New York: Grune & Stratton.

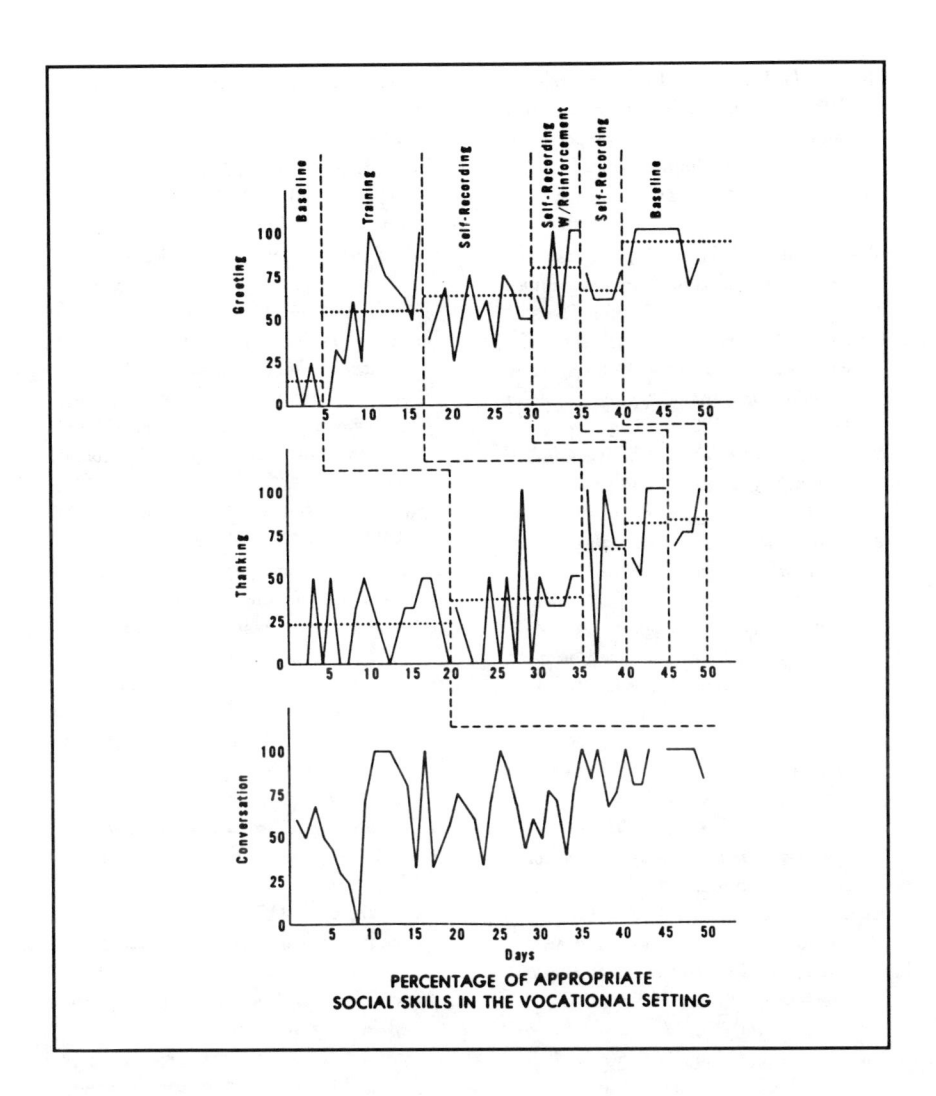

Figure 3. Percentage of greeting, thanking, and conversational skills displayed in the vocational setting.

Goldstein, A. P., Sprafkin, R. P., Gershaw, W. J., & Klein, P. (1983). Structured learning: A psychoeducational approach for teaching social competencies. *Behavioral Disorders, 8,* 161-170.

Gresham, F. M. (1981). Social skills training with handicapped children: A review. *Review of Educational Research, 51,* 139-176.

Gresham, F. M., & Nagle, R. J. (1980). Social skills training with children: Responsiveness to modeling and coaching as a function of peer orientation. *Journal of Consulting and Clinical Psychology, 18,* 718-729.

Kazdin, A. E. (1982). *Single-case research designs.* New York: Oxford Press.

Kochany, K., & Keifer, J. (1980). An analysis and evaluation of the failures of severely disabled individuals in competitive employment. In P. Wehman & M. Hill (Eds.), *Vocational training and placement of severely disabled persons.* Richmond: Virginia Commonwealth University.

Marburg, C. C., Houston, B. K., & Holmes, D. S. (1976). Influence of multiple models on the behavior of institutionalized retarded: Increased generalization to other models and other behaviors. *Journal of Consulting and Clinical Psychology, 44,* 514-519.

Mayhew, G. L., Enyart, P., & Anderson, J. (1978). Social reinforcement and the naturally occurring social responses of severely and profoundly retarded adolescents. *American Journal of Mental Deficiency, 83,* 164-170.

Meichenbaum, O. H. (1977). *Cognitive-behavior modification: An integrative approach.* New York: Plenum Press.

O'Connor, R. D. (1969). Modification of social withdrawal through systematic modeling. *Journal of Applied Behavior Analysis, 2,* 15-22.

O'Connor, R. D. (1972). Relative efficacy of modeling, shaping, and the combined procedures for modification of social withdrawal. *Journal of Abnormal Psychology, 79,* 327-334.

O'Leary, S. G., & Dubey, D. R. (1979). Applications of self-control procedures by children: A review. *Journal of Applied Behavior Analysis, 12,* 449-466.

Repp, A. C. (1979). Describing and monitoring behavior. In D. A. Sabatino & T. L. Miller (Eds.), *Describing learning characteristics of handicapped children and youth.* New York: Grune & Stratton.

Rusch, F.R., & Kazdin, A. E. (1981). Toward a methodology of withdrawal designs for the assessment of response maintenance. *Journal of Applied Behavior Analysis, 14,* 131-140.

Shores, R. E., Hester, P., & Strain, P. S. (1976). Effects of amount and type of teacher-child interaction on child-child interaction during free-play. *Psychology in the Schools, 13,* 171-175.

Strain, P. S., & Timm, M. A. (1974). An experimental analysis of social interaction between a behaviorally disordered preschool child and her classroom peers. *Journal of Applied Behavior Analysis, 7,* 583-590.

Turkewitz, H. K., O'Leary, D., & Ironsmith, M. (1975). Generalization and maintenance of appropriate behavior through self-control. *Journal of Consulting and Clinical Psychology, 43,* 577-583.

Walker, H., Greenwood, C., Hops, H., & Todd, N. (1979). Differential effects of reinforcing topographic components of social interaction: Analysis and systematic replication. *Behavior Modification, 3,* 291-321.

Warrenfeltz, R. B., Kelly, W. J., Salzberg, C. L., Beegle, C. P., Levy, S. M., Adams, T. A., & Crouse, T. R. (1981). Social skills training of behaviorally disordered adolescents with self-monitoring to promote generalization to a vocational setting. *Behavioral Disorders, 7,* 18-27.

Workman, E. A. (1982). *Teaching behavioral self-control to students.* Austin, TX: Pro-Ed.

Zahavi, S. L., & Asher, S. R. (1978). The effect of verbal instructions on preschool children's aggressive behavior. *Journal of School Psychology, 16,* 146-153.

APPENDIX

Behavioral Definitions of the Targeted Social Skills

Greeting

1. The student responded to or initiated a greeting (i.e., hi, hello) 5 sec after an opportunity. (An opportunity was defined as when a person passed him in the hallway or while he walked to the educational center, or when a different person entered his environment within a distance of approximately 3 feet while no other persons were between him and the person new to the environment.)
2. He made eye contact with the person he was greeting.
3. The student greeted the individual with a smile.
4. He used a moderate tone of voice.
5. He offered a greeting when the person was not already engaged in a conversation.
6. The student said the greeting only once.
7. He offered to shake the other person's hand.

Thanking

1. The student said "thank you" 5 sec after an opportunity. (An opportunity was defined as after being complimented or praised, after a request or favor was granted, or after a gift had been given to the student.)
2. The student said "thank you" in a friendly way.
3. He used a moderate tone of voice.
4. The student made eye contact with the individual he was thanking.
5. The subject thanked the person only once.

Initiating Conversation

1. The student initiated conversation (i.e., "It's a nice day today," "What did you do this weekend?"), and "Did you see the movie this weekend?" 10 sec after an opportunity. (An opportunity was defined as when a person was within 3 feet of the student with no other persons between him and the person. To be considered an opportunity the other person must not already be engaged in a conversation [i.e., the person might be sitting by the student or walking by the student].)
2. The student made eye contact.
3. He used a moderate tone of voice.
4. The student made content-appropriate statements.
5. He made the initiation statement only once.

Other Professional Development Products from The Council for Children with Behavioral Disorders

The Mini-Library Series on Emotional/Behavioral Disorders

Edited by Lyndal M. Bullock and Robert A. Gable

- *Best Practices for Managing the Behavior of Adolescents with Emotional/Behavioral Disorders Within the School Environment*
  Beverley H. Johns, Eleanor C. Guetzloe, Mitchell Yell, Brenda Scheuermann, Jo Webber, Valerie G. Carr, and Carl R. Smith
  Stock No. D5130, ISBN 0-86586-265-6, 1996, 48 pp.

- *Developing a System of Care: Interagency Collaboration for Students with Emotional/Behavioral Disorders*
  Russell Skiba, Lewis Polsgrove, and Karen Nasstrom
  Stock No. D5131, ISBN 0-86586-266-4, 1996, 56 pp.

- *Early Intervention for Young Children At Risk for Emotional/Behavioral Disorders: Implications for Policy and Practice*
  Wesley Brown, Maureen A. Conroy, James J. Fox, Joseph Wehby, Carol Davis, and Mary McEvoy
  Stock No. D5132, ISBN 0-86586-267-2, 1996, 40 pp.

- *Effective Strategies for Teaching Appropriate Behaviors to Children With Emotional/Behavioral Disorders*
  Robert B. Rutherford, Jr., Mary M. Quinn, and Sarup R. Mathur
  Stock No. D5133, ISBN 0-86586-268-0, 1996, 48 pp.

- *Planning and Implementing Effective Programs for School-Aged Children and Youth with Emotional/Behavioral Disorders Within Inclusive Schools*
  Howard S. Muscott, Daniel P. Morgan, and Nancy B. Meadows
  Stock No. D5134, ISBN 0-86586-269-9, 1996, 56 pp.

- *Teacher-Mediated Behavior Management Strategies for Children With Emotional/Behavioral Disorders*
  Sarup R. Mathur, Mary M. Quinn, Robert B. Rutherford, Jr.
  Stock No. D5135, ISBN 0-86586-270-2, 1996, 48 pp.

- *Types of Youth Aggression and Violence and Implications for Prevention and Treatment*
  Richard Van Acker
  Stock No. D5136, ISBN 0-86586-271-0, 1996, 48 pp.

Save 10% by ordering the entire library, Stock No. D5137, 1996. For the most current price information or to order

Call 1-800-CEC-READ (232-7323) or FAX 703-264-1637

The Council for Exceptional Children
1920 Association Drive • Reston, VA 22091-1589